Forbidden SOLDIER

Alexander (Alex) Khan was born in Scotland in 1975 to mixed-race parents. He spent most of his early years living in North West England. Alex joined the British Army in 1996.

He spent 2 years of his military career working as an Assistant Skydiving Instructor at the 'Joint Service Parachute Centre,' in Germany, and as a display jumper on the Royal Artillery Parachute Team.

He was deployed to Kuwait before sent to Iraq in March 2003. After 7 years, Alex left the Army.

He now runs his own telecommunication business and lives with his wife and son in Hampshire.

Alexander Khan's first book, *Orphan of Islam*, described how his young life fell apart when his Asian father died suddenly and his English mother disappeared without trace. Alex was sent to Pakistan to be re-educated, but he escaped the clutches of the fundamentalists and returned to England.

This is where *Orphan of Islam* ended. As well as hundreds of rave reviews for the book, readers were keen to know what happened next. Finally, this long-awaited story can be told and, if anything, it is even more dramatic than *Orphan of Islam*.

BOOKS by Alexander Khan

Non-Fiction

Orphan of Islam
Forbidden SOLDIER

Fiction (short stories)

The Recruit
Act of Vengeance

Forbidden SOLDIER

A Remarkable True Story of Survival, Courage and Hope

Alexander Khan

This is a work of non-fiction. However, the names and identities of some of the people and places in the book have been disguised to respect and protect their privacy.

Everything else has been described as it happened.

Contents

Also includes:

The Recruit   Chapter One & Chapter Two
Act of Vengeance   Chapter One & Chapter Two

7th Parachute Regiment RHA History

Dedication

I dedicate this novella to my wife Jessica and my two boys Zachary and Joshua.

Introduction

This story is the sequel to *Orphan of Islam*, the book I wrote about my life up to the age of 17 that was published by Harper Collins in July 2012. In that book, I detailed what it was like to grow up as a mixed-race child of a Pakistani father and a white English mother in 1970s and 1980s Lancashire, England. Readers of the book will know that my mother disappeared from my life very early on, and that my sister and I were raised by a conservative religious family in harsh conditions following the sudden death of my father.

Orphan of Islam describes how I was sent to Pakistan to be educated in a madrassa and how I escaped from there, eventually making my way back to England after witnessing an killing.

I had hoped to tell the story of what happened to me next within the pages of '*Orphan...*' but for various reasons this didn't happen. '*Orphan...*' has received many, many great reviews but a lot of those praising the book also confessed to feeling disappointed that the ending didn't quite resolve in the way they'd hoped. I agreed with their viewpoint, which is why I planned to write a follow-up soon after '*Orphan...*' was published but as usual, life got in the way.

At that stage perhaps it's just as well that it did, because life has changed enormously for me since 2012 and in a sense, things have come full circle. The coronavirus pandemic and subsequent lockdown gave me time to think about everything that happened to me post-17 and somehow the time seemed right to revisit my past and talk about the events that led me to where I am now.

Forbidden Soldier

For those of you not familiar with my story, it may be useful to read *Orphan of Islam* before starting out with *Forbidden SOLDIER*. However, it isn't entirely necessary. Below I will give a summary of what happened to me up to the age of 17 and as this book progresses I will refer to events detailed in *'Orphan..'*. Should you wish to know more about these particular events, this might be the time to delve into the book.

At the age of 17 I returned from Pakistan to my home town in Lancashire, which I have called Hawesmill. It's typical of many former mill towns in East Lancashire; largely poor and run-down, with various social problems connected to unemployment, health, housing and ethnicity. This last factor played a big part in my early life; I was both Asian and white, and in a place like Hawesmill where you're most definitely either one or the other, I was the odd one out, always looking for a place I could call home. In many ways, I still am.

My parents, Ahmed and Margaret, met in the late 1960s when they were working in a mill. They moved away from Lancashire to Scotland, hoping to make a new start in a less judgemental environment. I was born in Dundee and named Moham Khan.

Eventually my parents returned to the North West of England but there were problems and when I was three my sister Jasmine and I were taken to Pakistan by my father. At this point our mother completely disappeared from our lives.

After three years in Pakistan we returned to Hawesmill, lodging with Fatima, my father's sister.

Soon we discovered that my father had another family in Pakistan, who later came to join us.

Life began to settle down, albeit I always wondered about and missed my mother.

When I was ten my father died suddenly and from then on we would be raised by my stepmother along with her cruel, bullying brother Rafiq. This individual picked on me mercilessly. Nothing I did was ever good enough for him and for a couple of years I endured his bullying until he duped me into 'visiting' relatives in Pakistan – on a one-way ticket. Apparently I was to be re-educated until I became an exemplary Muslim. What I didn't know then was that this would include a spell in a madrassa – a fundamentalist Islamic college on the Pakistan-Afghanistan border.

Somehow I escaped this place and after a series of adventures I returned to the village I'd been billeted at with my Pakistani family. I was lucky not to be sent straight back but, having then been promised in marriage to a family member who was nothing more than a child, it was clear I'd never be going back to Britain. That was until I witnessed a shocking and horrific honour killing perpetrated by a cousin and almost immediately afterwards I was on a flight home, away from the probing questions of the Pakistani police.

Back in the UK the prospect of an arranged marriage still loomed over me. However, I had other ideas. I fell in with a gang of boys who semi-squatted a derelict house in Hawesmill and although we became close friends it was clear by then that we were going our separate ways.

They were talking of jihad and training camps and Afghanistan, while I…well, I never wanted to see or hear about that place again.

When they left, to do whatever they were going to do, I found myself alone, which is where *Orphan of Islam* ends.

Actually, that isn't quite true. I wrote a short epilogue which cryptically let the reader know that at last I'd found my mother and that we were about to be reunited. This was the source of a lot of readers' disappointment. Quite rightly, they wanted to know how and why this happened, and what had gone on in the intervening years. Finally, I'm now able to reveal all.

Looking back at the paragraphs above which outline my story, I find it hard to believe that these things happened to me. By the age of 17 you'd be forgiven for thinking that I'd had enough experiences to last a lifetime. Little did I know there was a lot more to come...

Please enjoy this book, and if you were one of those who wanted a more conclusive ending to 'Orphan...' I hope that I've delivered it for you. In life, not everything ends happily but if it ends well, sometimes that's as much as we can expect.

The struggle you're in today is developing the strength you
need for tomorrow.
Robert Tew

Forbidden Soldier

Chapter One

A sniffers lair

Forbidden Soldier

A beautiful summer's day; a rarity for this part of North West England. July here is often wet and cold, along with the other eleven months of the year. This damp climate was the reason the cotton industry came to Lancashire in the Industrial Revolution, the soggy air binding together the raw fibres to be spun into thread and fabric. Many years later, people from south Asia would move into the tiny terraced houses once occupied by English mill workers and find employment in that dying industry. When it disappeared, a sub-culture of 'Indian' restaurants, takeaways and taxi-driving would sustain this insular community, but only just.

My dad, Ahmed, is pushing me on the swing in the local park. He is a part of the Pakistani community who have made their lives far from home in Hawesmill. My mum is here too; white British, and a local girl who has taken the bold step of marrying a person still being commonly described as a 'Paki'.

Her own community have shunned her for doing so, and my dad's relatives aren't too pleased either. Still, they've defied the odds, staying together and having two children: me and my sister Jasmine.

Today we're a happy family, trying to catch tiddlers from the narrow stream which runs through the park and playing 'catch' on the grass. Mum extracts samosas from a clear plastic box while dad puffs and pants as he pushes me harder so that I will reach higher, and higher, and higher...

But the dream is gone, washed away by the incessant rain which taps on the grimy window of a cold bedroom in a damp, derelict house. I am alone, lying on a grubby mattress with only a coat to cover me. Waking up, I blink and for a moment wonder where my idyllic surroundings have gone to. Where is the warmth and freedom of this joyful and sunny day? Where is the park, the swings and the river? Above all, where are Mum, Dad and Jasmine?

I knew where my sister was. At just 17 years old, she was fretting over the prospect of an arranged marriage to a man in Yorkshire she had never met. She knew what would be expected of her; a life of cooking, cleaning and child-rearing. She would swap one set of bleak terraced streets for another across the Pennines, the pattern of her existence woven into permanent shape.

I also knew where Dad was – lying under a heap of rocks and dirt in a Pakistani graveyard. Dead before he was 50 of a smoking-related heart attack. Mum was also dead, or so I'd been told. I'd never quite believed it, of course, but it had been a convenient tale to tell two young, bewildered orphans who were about to be taken in by Dad's family and subjected to a life which, beyond the paint-worn door of 97 Nile Street, was exclusively Pakistani and Muslim. Mum being 'dead' was useful; there needn't be any focus on our 'other' heritage and the family were free to mould us the way they wanted.

At this stage in my life, aged 17 or so, I'd been through

that religious mill and had come out the other side battered and bruised.

I'd been beaten for not going to the mosque, and beaten again because I had been but hadn't understood what the imam was saying. I'd been sent to Pakistan, ending up in a fundamentalist madrassa (Islamic school) run by fanatical jihadists.

I ran away from there and despite the odds, wasn't sent back – but only because I'd witnessed a vicious and horrific honour killing at close quarters. Immediately after I was returned to England and back into the clutches of Dad's family.

At this age, however, I was becoming too old for them to control and gradually I drifted into a world of doss houses, weed, booze and boastful talk of waging jihad against the *kuffar* (unbeliever). My wayward friends Hamid, Bashir and Azam had already done just that, spiriting themselves away to Pakistan, from where they would eventually join ex-mujahideen fighters in a new organisation – the Taliban. I wanted no part of that. I'd already spent time with such people while imprisoned in the madrassa and I hadn't liked what I'd seen.

With my pale skin and reputation for the trouble and shame I'd brought on my family, particularly my 'Uncle' Rafiq and my father's sister, Aunty Fatima, I was the talk of the neighbourhood and although I tried to keep a low profile I stood out like a sore thumb.

Everywhere I went there were whispers and sideways glances. I was the *kuffar*, the part-white unbeliever who had been sent to Pakistan to learn how to be a good Muslim and had come back twice as bad.

I slunk around the streets and alleyways of Hawesmill, weaving through Nile Street, where we'd lived as kids when Dad was alive and the world didn't seem such a dangerous place, and dodging Hamilton Terrace, where the violent Rafiq still lived. His hatred of me knew no bounds and even if I'd spent a day successfully managing to dodge him, I would still crawl back to my damp bedroom with his peculiarly pronounced name for me, 'Bastarrd!' rolling around in my head.

One place I could visit without too much interference was the mosque in Sebastopol Street. Despite everything, at this stage I was still religiously observant and would make every effort to attend the required five times a day. I didn't always manage it, but whenever I did it was in the knowledge that however many evil looks Rafiq threw me from the far side of the room, he could never physically do anything to me in there which would offend God.

Even so, the prayers and sermons I'd grown up with as a child, before Pakistan beckoned, were very different to those I was hearing now. In the past, the talk had been one of Islam as a religion of peace and tolerance. The verses we heard (at least those I understood, or that were explained to me) were poetic and beautiful. Not any longer. Now, in the early 1990s and following the controversy over

Salman Rushdie's book *The Satanic Verses*, the message coming from the mosques of northern England was far more militant. There was anger and upset, and talk of revenge in the air. The religion of peace became something far more hard-line and intolerant, and this didn't stay solely in the mosques. On the streets, boys I knew who were never seen in anything else other than T-shirt and jeans now wore full salwar kameez and were trying desperately to grow bushy beards. Gradually, more and more girls were appearing in hijabs, some of them wearing full face coverings. A change had come over the Asian community in Hawesmill, and it was one being replicated all over the north of England and beyond. It was a holy war for the soul of Islam, and the hardliners were definitely winning.

I was still being threatened with the prospect of an arranged marriage (for 'arranged' let's say 'forced') to Parveen, a young girl I'd been introduced to while in Pakistan.

She was no more than a child and the thought of making a home and having a family with someone who was barely out of the playing-with-dolls stage sickened me. Even so, whenever I did see Rafiq he would challenge me directly about it.

"Hey, you...bastarrd...you know what's waiting for you, don't you? We're watching you, every moment of the day. You'll marry that girl, bastarrd, whether you like it or not." Then he'd flash me that evil smile.

"You're gonna do it...Your sister's doing it, isn't she, bastarrd? So why not you?"

I couldn't answer. I'd had phone conversations with Jasmine, who told me she would be married off very soon. She was about to turn 18 and although she said she didn't want to marry anyone, at least not now, she had no choice. A guy in Yorkshire had been lined up for her and that seemed to be that.

"I wish Mum was around to help us, Mo," she said.

"We always say that, don't we? No sign of her though, is there?"

"Have you been looking?" Jasmine asked.

I was always looking. Searching, searching, searching. Scanning the faces of the white women I passed in the street, gazing out of minibus windows wet with condensation during occasional trips to other mosques in Blackburn, Preston, Oldham and Bradford. Wondering if I might spot someone passing by who might bear a fleeting resemblance to Mum, what I could remember of her. Which in truth, was very little. Long dark hair and a white face. Not a lot to go on.

This search very often took me into town, beyond Hawesmill's narrow confines.

There was nothing much to do there, but at least I wasn't hiding from every hostile face leering at me in those crowded streets. What did attract me were the bright lights of a town centre amusement arcade and, armed with the few quid I earned from deliveries or working off and on in the local shop, I'd spent hours in there, playing the machines while keeping out of the cold and wet. One day, I noticed a girl looking at me. She was white, about 17 or 18, and with cute freckles across her nose. Embarrassed, I looked away, but when I glanced back she was still staring over. And now she was smiling... I returned the smile and within minutes we were chatting. She was called Helen, and she came from the better end of town, a part I'd heard of but never visited.

We were both naïve and, in our own ways, very vulnerable. We clung to one another first as friends but very quickly, as lovers. And we were young – far too young for what inevitably occurred. Helen became pregnant within weeks of us meeting and nine months later we had a son.
We moved in together in an attempt to make something of a family life. Looking back, we were silly to
think that two kids could raise a baby on their own.

But we tried. I got a job in a takeaway, working all hours, while Helen stayed at home and did her best to be a good mum. However, it wasn't long before the strain began to show.

Helen got stick from people criticising her for having a baby with a 'Paki', while my family demanded that I leave her, go home, and marry the girl I was promised to in Pakistan. Once again I was piggy in the middle, caught between two cultures and not belonging to either.

Most of Hawesmill knew that I'd gone a bit wild since coming back from Afghanistan.

Only a trusted few knew that I'd got together with a white lass from the other side of town, the posh end where no Asians other than taxi drivers ever visited. It was only a 20-minute walk from Hawesmill, but it could've been the other side of the world.

I knew it would be different with a white girl, but not this different. From a young age I'd been intrigued by white people. I wondered what they ate, how they smelled, what they did in the evening, how they talked to one another – everything. Being half-white, this level of interest wasn't surprising. I clamoured to know more about the culture that had abandoned me, and which was so fiercely denied to me by my Muslim family.

When we first moved in together I was fascinated – and disturbed – by Helen's habit of cooking bacon and sausages for breakfast most mornings. Pork is strictly *haram* (forbidden) in the Muslim culture and even the smell of it aroused deep feelings of guilt and fear in me.

But I wasn't going to stop Helen from eating it. Things were different now, and I promised I'd be as tolerant and understanding as I could.

At last I had a real family to care for, and I wouldn't do anything to jeopardise that.

This was a challenging time for both of us, but at least I could get out of the house for a breather. For Helen, it was different. Soon she realised how trapped she was, and how much extra support she needed.

I guess I should've seen it coming but I was too wrapped up in my efforts to make the situation work.

She wanted to spend time with friends. Of course she did, she was only a teenager, but instead of understanding the situation and trying to work out a compromise, I became jealous and possessive.

She began to spend nights at her mum's house, taking the baby with her. Finally, she asked me to leave. I tried to argue but it was hopeless. Helen knew her own mind and she figured she could do this without me around, making the situation more difficult.

I had no choice but to walk away. As the door closed behind me, I realised I'd gone from being a family man with a partner and a baby to....well, to what? An 'ex'? Most definitely. An idiot? I certainly felt that way. A homeless person?

I stopped in my tracks. Where would I go now? I couldn't go back to Hawesmill, that was for sure. I'd have been torn apart by Rafiq and the rest of the family. And I'd brought so much shame on them by now they wouldn't want me anyway. I'd no friends at the takeaway – they'd heard about my relationship and only tolerated me because I was an extra pair of hands. They'd soon find someone else to take my job, when it became obvious I was too dirty and tired to do it.

I wandered into the park and sat on the bench, a black bin liner filled with a few possessions between my knees.

So this was homelessness. Desperately I tried to think of cousins or mates who might let me stay a night or two, while I got sorted. It was a short list, and when I got to the end I knew I was stuck. The relatives wouldn't touch me with a bargepole and my friends were all away in Pakistan.

It was early autumn and the nights were getting chilly. I could sit on this bench all night, trying to work out what to do, or I could just start walking and see what turned up.

Instinctively I set off in the direction of Hawesmill, even though I knew the dangers of being spotted by Rafiq or his friends.

Whatever that place was, it was the closest to what I knew as 'home'. As I walked, I thought about a youth club for local kids in Earlston, another area of terraced housing close to Hawesmill, but with a more mixed population. As well as Pathans, Punjabis and Bangladeshis lads attended, along with the very occasional white kid. The youth workers were all Asian and the few times I'd been there I'd found them to be kind and helpful. Maybe they knew a place I could doss down for a night or two?

I turned on to the canal towpath, which I knew would lead me straight to Earlston. After half a mile or so I came to an old bridge over the canal. If I went up the steps at the side of the bridge and across the road I would be at the youth centre. Easy. But not this night. Under the bridge I could make out a group of shadowy figures, huddled together, their baseball caps pulled down over their eyes.

I thought back to when I was about 12, and the beating I got from two white lads lurking under a road bridge who jumped me as I returned home from mosque.

The lads under the canal bridge looked hard, and even though they were Asian – their accents a dead giveaway –

there was nothing stopping them giving a good hiding to a stranger like me or worse, throwing me in the canal. I screwed my fists into a ball and waited for the inevitable challenge. It wasn't long in coming.

"Oi, lad! Where are you going, then?"

The leader stepped out in front of me, blocking my way. The whites of his eyes were bloodshot and he was swaying slightly. He looked hard into my face and spoke to me in English.

"I know you, don't I? You work in the takeaway."

"Used to."

"What happened? Shit in the food, did you?"

The others laughed; weird, hollow splutters and grunts that didn't sound real. I knew enough by now to know these lads were on something. It didn't think it was alcohol, but I suspected cannabis, even though I couldn't smell the tell-tale pungent aroma of burning hash.

The leader's face softened. "So where are you going now?" he asked.

"Dunno."

"You can hang around with us if you want." He produced a small yellow tin from his coat pocket.

"Wanna sniff?"

Now, I was 19 and there'd been a couple of occasions I'd smoked joints with Bashir and friends before they went to Pakistan. I'd never been entirely comfortable with it, even if the others smoked it like it was growing wild around Hawesmill, but it didn't seem to affect me much. So when this hard-looking, baseball-capped lad shoved a tin of strong-smelling liquid under my nose and almost commanded me to have a go, I accepted, thinking I knew everything about drugs.

"Just pour some into the cap and sniff it in," he said, looking at me like I was dumb.

To this day I don't know why I didn't walk off. Perhaps it was because these boys didn't seem as hostile as I initially thought. Maybe, deep down, I knew I was seeking oblivion from everything going on around me. Whatever the reason, I did as I was told. Within seconds my head was spinning and I felt panicky and sick.

I squatted down against the curved stone wall of the bridge and put my head between my knees. I could hear them laughing, but it sounded like they were miles away.

The damp, stony smell of the towpath mixed with a more subtle fragrance of moss and lichen on the wall I was leaning against. My mind struggled to keep up with my thoughts, one image melting into another, a running commentary mixing up English and Pathan, everything exploding into chaos. After five minutes or so this rush wore off, replaced by a deep feeling of peaceful calm, like the best dream you've ever had, except awake.

For most of that evening I sniffed lighter fuel with these guys, who'd suddenly become my new best mates. Now, I see they must all have been outsiders, rebels in one form or another, cast out by their families for bringing shame on them and the community. In that sense, I was one of them, and the more I inhaled the intoxicant the more I bonded with them.

The following morning I woke up on a soggy, sagging mattress in what appeared to be a near derelict wooden shed. A couple of the lads I'd been with the previous night were also there, out to the world. God knows how we'd got there. In the semi-light I could see crusty, festering sores around their open mouths.

My head hurt like hell and I was cold. I staggered to my feet and look out of the grimy, cobweb-covered window. Beyond was what looked like a small park. I'd no idea where we were, and could only guess this was some kind of disused workmen's hut. A few meagre possessions were scattered about.

A bent pan with a few hard baked beans soldered to its base sat on a small camping stove.

Tins of butane were everywhere. A sniffers' lair. I lay down again, on my back, and tried to piece together the events of the previous evening. I felt like shit, and I wondered what time the lads would wake up. I was desperate for another go of the gas. It was the beginning of a slow descent into darkness.

When you're at the end of your rope, tie a knot and hold on.
Theodore Roosevelt

Forbidden Soldier

Chapter Two

To my shame and my pain

Forbidden Soldier

For months I carried on this way; solvent sniffing, drinking, weed-smoking and dossing down wherever I could. Every day I obliterated thoughts of Helen and our son with whatever I could get my hands on.

I was in a spiral of hopelessness. Days and nights blended together and often I would wake up in some damp, mice-infested dump of a derelict house, the same sores around my mouth that I'd first seen on the sniffers I'd befriended under the bridge. Wayward thoughts drifted through my frazzled brain, only connected by whatever substance had induced them. Mum and Dad and Jasmine, the three of us in the park, playing on the swings. Then Dad's death, and the battering I received from Rafiq the night before the funeral...then Pakistan, the teachers at the madrassa and my failure to master the Qur'an in Arabic, to my shame and my pain.

Some thoughts would come and go while others would linger, nagging at me when I was awake and torturing me in my drug-addled dreams. Two in particular came back night after night; the sexual abuse I suffered in Pakistan at the hands of my cousin Farida and, worst of all, the honour killing carried out in front of me by my cousin Qaisar, the victim being his lively young wife Ayesha.

As I lay in a semi-conscious state on whatever filthy mattress I'd managed to drag back to my room, pools of blood congealing like strawberry jam appeared before me, accompanied by the most hideous screams.

Again and again I hallucinated the vision of poor Ayesha writhing on the dirt floor of Aunty Alia's kitchen, desperately trying to stem the flow of blood and brains from a gunshot wound to her head. Then I saw Qaisar raising the revolver once more and pumping shots into her to finish her off.

No matter how much booze I swallowed or solvent I sniffed, I couldn't shift these haunting visions. My waking moments were made worse by the knowledge that the family in Hawesmill now knew that I'd been with a white girl and fathered a son. In terms of living up to the community's expectations of a 'good Muslim' I was hardly a poster boy to begin with, but now my disgrace was complete. Jasmine managed to get a message to me, via a friend, that I'd been rumbled and once again I was a marked man. We arranged a telephone call – not easy when all that was available was a piss-sodden red telephone box which might or might not be working, and no guarantee that my poor repressed sister would even be able to turn up.

Luckily, she managed to sneak out of the house by pretending to go to the chemist, and without being spotted dodged into the phone box at the bottom of Nile Street. She rang the number she'd been given, connecting her to another phone box in town.

"Mo?" she said, her voice full of fear. How did she know she hadn't been set up by someone out to get me?

"It's me," I replied. "How are you?"

"I'm OK," she said, "sort of."

"I want to see you, Jasmine." It was true. I hadn't seen my sister for months and I wanted one final get-together with her before she was married off and disappeared over the Pennines.

"You can't," she said. "There's no way. You can't hang around up here. They'll find you."

"Who will find me? Them? I don't care if they do."

By this stage I was past caring what happened to me. My mind was too far gone to sense any lurking dangers. All that interested me was getting out of my head, as often as possible. If someone – Rafiq, for example – caught me and punched me in the face, well, so what? Any pain he could give me physically was nothing compared to the ache and grief I felt inside.

"You will care," she said. "You'll care a lot if he gets hold of you."

"Rafiq? I couldn't give a shit about him."

"Well, you should do. You need to wake up, Mo. They're onto you. They want you out of the way again. They're planning something."

"Like what?"

"I don't know, they won't tell me and they go quiet when I'm around. But they're up to something."

"I don't care."

"Mo, this is serious. I think it might be Pakistan for you. And this time you won't be coming back."

The urgency in her voice suddenly shook me out of my nonchalance. Pakistan? Surely not again. And if the plan were to send me there on a one-way ticket, what would happen to me while I was there? They knew I was capable of escaping situations – maybe this time they'd make sure there was no escape for me, just like poor Ayesha.

The weeks went by and I was still drugging it, nodding out in local parks and crawling back to whatever passed for 'home'. But Jasmine's words had stirred something in me. I knew how easy it was to spirit someone out of the country.

It had happened to me before and I'd gone along with it like a lamb to the slaughter. OK, I was older now and not as suggestible, but these people could be clever when they wanted to make something happen. With the right kind of flattery, I knew I could easily find myself at Heathrow Airport again, boarding a flight to Islamabad, and God knows what.

Off and on I'd been away from the house in Hamilton Terrace for about three years. Over that time I'd occasionally gone back, mostly when I'd been dragged there by family members. These were the times I'd fought back and received a severe beating in return. I'd got to the stage where I was past caring what they thought about me, but I certainly didn't want to be shipped back to Pakistan. I sat for many hours staring into space, wondering what would become of me and whether or not I really cared enough about myself to get out of this situation.

Around this time a couple of things happened that would give me the faintest spark of hope. The first was the discovery of an old portable TV in the house I was squatting in and amazingly it worked. Finally I had something to focus on other than my own mind and I spent hours each evening watching any old rubbish to divert myself from booze and drugs.

In those days you had to sit through the adverts, and one which hooked me was a recruitment ad for the British Army. Tough-looking guys were travelling in jeeps, trekking across moorland and attacking targets at night in full camouflage gear. The more I saw it the more I was intrigued. These young blokes looked like they belonged to a tight unit; a family, almost. They stood shoulder to shoulder against whatever was being thrown at them, and whatever didn't kill them seemed to make them stronger.

Their world seemed a million miles away from mine, and yet I felt drawn to what they were offering. I didn't know anything about the British Army, other than they were the ones who policed the Empire, including in India, and in some ways a lad like me with Pakistani heritage should've seen them as the natural enemy, like so many of my mates did. But I just couldn't view British soldiers that way. To me, there was something honourable about them; even in the toughest circumstances these guys hung together and made it through.

It appealed to me – until I took a look in the mirror. I was out of condition, a knackered-looking, drugged-up slob. How could I ever imagine I'd be accepted into the British Army? The lads in the advert looked like they could move mountains. I could barely move out of bed. The idea was appealing, yes, but I decided it wasn't for me. They'd take one look at me and send me straight home again. Besides, whoever saw any 'Pakis' in the British Army?

The second took place on the canal which runs through the town. I often walked along the towpath, staring into the water to see if it could give me answers to my many problems.

By now it was late 1995 and the clouds drifting across the Pennines were as grey and forbidding as the canal itself.

I picked up a few stones from the towpath and skimmed them across the water, hoping they'd reach the other bank without disappearing into the depths. Then from about 20 yards away I heard a voice shout in my direction.

"Oi, dickhead! Stop that, will ya?! You're gonna frighten t'fish off!"

I looked over to see a white lad roughly the same age as me, sitting on a box that was facing the water.

With a rod in his hand and a beanie on his head he looked like a garden gnome.

He also looked as hard as nails. Immediately I dropped the stones and stared at him.

"What are you lookin' at, lad?" he said, standing up.

"Nowt," I replied. "It's just that I didn't think there were any fish in here. Too polluted, I've heard."

"Used to be," he said, "when I come down here with my dad when I were a kid. S'alright now though. See…"

He pointed to a long net that was mostly submerged in the water, before pulling it up to show me the contents. I could see about half a dozen silver-bellied fish, writhing and gasping as they emerged from the murk.

"Bloody hell, not bad!"

"Usually it's more than that," he said. "It's a quiet day."

"I've never been fishing before," I said.

He looked at me closely. "I'm not surprised," he said. "You lot never… Sorry, I don't mean it like that. It's just…well you don't, do you?"

"My mum's white," I replied, "but yeah, we don't go fishing. We don't have time for hobbies or owt really."

"Too busy working?"

"And praying. It's just the way it is. What's your name?"

"Jamie. What's yours?"

"Mo."

He laughed. "Shoulda guessed, shouldn't I? Come here. I'll show you what it's about."

For the next hour or so I squatted next to Jamie as he showed me how you slide a small wooden float up the fishing line, then attach a hook to the end before squeezing on three or four tiny lead weights. I shuddered as he took a fat white maggot from a plastic box and hooked it on.

"You'll have to get used to that if you want to do fishing," he said, grinning.

Then he raised his arm and cast the line into the water.

"What happens now?" I asked.

"We wait. If the float suddenly goes under the water that means a fish has taken the bait. When that happens I pull the rod up quick. It's called a 'strike'. The hook goes into the fish's mouth and we've got him. That's the idea."

The float turned upright and gently waggled in the breeze which cut across the water. Jamie asked where I was from, what I did. I told him a few things, but keeping the finer details to myself. He mentioned he was from a town up the road, a place I'd never visited.

"Don't get out much, do yer?" he said.

"Nah…I've done all the travelling I need to do for the time being."

"Oh aye? Where've you been then?"

Before I could answer something caught Jamie's eye and, lightning fast, he snatched up the rod and pulled hard. The line shook furiously, bending the tip of the rod towards the water.

"We're on!" he said, grinning.

For the next couple of minutes I watched as Jamie skilfully played the thrashing fish towards the net. Flashes of silver, green and red erupted from the water as the fish twisted this way and that to escape the hook. Eventually, the fight all spent, Jamie slid a net attached to a long pole under the fish and lifted it from the canal.

"Nice perch," he said, unhooking it and holding it out towards me. I'd never seen a live fish before and was impressed by its large, spiky dorsal fin and vivid black stripes along its body.

"I didn't think fish like that lived in here," I said. "Can you eat it?"

Jamie laughed. "You could try," he said, "but all you'll taste is mud and bones."

We chatted for a while longer until I realised Jamie might want some time on his own. Fishermen always seemed to be alone, I'd noticed. I got up to leave.

"You off then?" Jamie said.

"Yeah. I'll leave you in peace. Cheers for showing me about fishing."

"S'alright...I'll be here again on Wednesday, if you wanna meet up or owt?"

I nodded. "Nice one. I'd like that. See you next week then."

I walked away smiling. Something about Jamie's brash but kind nature appealed to me. As I've mentioned, I'd always wondered about white people; how they lived, what their houses looked like, what they ate, how they talked to each other.

That part of my heritage had been sorely missing and although I'd had some experience of it with Helen and her family, I still felt very awkward about entering their world.

With Jamie it was different and as the weeks went by and we met up on the canal bank, we discovered we were becoming friends. Not in so many words – young northern lads don't tend to dwell on the nature of friendship – but in actions and a natural closeness which developed between the two of us.

Eventually, Jamie invited me to meet his family. He lived with his mum in a terraced house like the ones in Hawesmill, but a lot less run-down and much more cared for. Straight away I sensed a warm and loving family atmosphere within their walls, an atmosphere I'd never noticed in Hamilton Terrace.

I was particularly struck by Jamie's mum, a slim woman with long, dark hair who straight away reminded me of the vision of my mother; a person I'd barely known who'd haunted my dreams for so many years.

Immediately she was kind and loving towards me, so much so that I imagined that she could be my long-lost mum, and this is how it would be had she stayed, and we'd experienced a normal family existence.

Then I met Steve, Jamie's brother. Jamie had talked about him, but had been a bit coy about what he did for a living. One day when I was round at Jamie's he turned up at the door, home on leave.

Every inch of him shouted 'military'. His shoes were clean, his clothes were neat and ironed and he stood tall. He had an inner confidence you could almost taste, yet he was probably only a couple of years older than me.

He'd been in the army since he was 18 and it showed. Yet he was a nice bloke too, not a show-off pretending to be a tough guy.

We sat and drank tea together and I listened in silence as he told us of some of the things he'd been up to. A tour of Cyprus, all sunshine and sailing, followed by a tense few months in Northern Ireland. I liked the fact that every tricky situation seemed to be followed by a laugh and a joke between Steve and his mates.

The more I heard, the more I liked the sound of this life. When I saw the TV advert I'd thought the army wasn't for me, but something about the way Steve spoke about it made me realise I might have been too quick to dismiss the idea. I asked him a few questions about joining up, fitness, pay – that sort of thing. I expected him to reply with something like, "Your lot aren't popular in the army", but instead he trained his gaze on me.

"Why are you asking, Mo? Are you thinking of giving it a go?"

"Well, I dunno, not sure if it's really me…" I replied.

"You don't know til you try," he said. "So why don't you give it a try?"

Now I was on the back foot. "Nah," I said. "They won't have me. Not my kind."

"Bollocks," said Steve firmly. "They'll have anyone, provided you're up for it, fit enough and like teamwork. Oh, and no nutters. Actually – scratch that. You have to be a nutter to get in!"

I laughed. Jamie looked at me. "Are you really up for it, Mo?" he said.

"It's a good life. You've heard it from our Steve. It's not for me, though. No going fishing in uniform!"

"Tell you what," said Steve, "I'm home for a few days. Why don't we go down the Army Careers Office down Blackburn, have a chat with the sergeant there? I know him, he's a good lad. He'll tell you the truth, then you can have a think about it. Alright?"

"Nice one," I said. "What've I got to lose?"

Don't worry about what I'm doing. Worry about why you're worried about what I'm doing.
Anonymous

Chapter Three

Sweat, garlic and cigarettes

Forbidden Soldier

I thought I could detect a slight smirk developing across the face of the recruiting sergeant as Steve and I walked into the Army Careers Office in early spring 1996. After several conversations with Steve I'd been persuaded to catch the bus into Blackburn and have a chat with his mate. It felt strange to be entering a place very far removed from the streets of Hawesmill and even as I got off the bus I looked round nervously, expecting someone from my community to have followed me, watching my every move.

"Who've we got here then, Steve?" the sergeant said, looking me up and down.

"This is Mo," Steve said. "He's a mate of our kid. We've been talking about joining the mob, haven't we, Mo?"

I nodded, feeling somewhat intimidated by the strapping six-footer in military uniform sizing me up.

"That right?" said the sergeant. "What makes you think you'll be a good recruit, Mo?"

I hadn't been expecting a question like that. I thought they'd ask me about flat feet or whether I liked crap food. I'd assumed joining the army would be easy. Maybe not...

"Erm...I dunno," I replied. "I've seen adverts on the telly and it looks like a laugh. I think I'd fit in well."

"Do you now?" the sergeant said, casting a glance at Steve. "You might have to be more certain than that, lad."

"Why?"

"Not many from your neck of the woods walk in here, if you know what I mean," he said. "You could come in for a bit of shit, you know."

"I'll be alright," I said. "I can look after myself."

"Right. So what would you do if someone kept making racist remarks? Trying to provoke you, like?"

"Names don't hurt me," I said. "It's their problem, not mine. I'd just get on with the job. Anyway, I won't know unless I join up, will I?"

The sergeant nodded. "True. How's your fitness?"

I'd been expecting this one. "Not brilliant at the moment," I admitted. "I've been having a rough time recently. But I want to shove all that behind me."

"I won't dick you around, Mo," said the sergeant. "You have to be the absolute best to join the army. We don't take just anyone these days. You need to show us more than just being able to breathe. And to be the best, you need to be 100 per cent fit. You won't last ten seconds otherwise."

He picked up some leaflets from the desk. "Here," he said, "have a look through these, see what you think. If you're still into joining up, come back in a couple of months."

He pointed at my growing pot-belly. "And if you do, I want to see that gone. A lad of your age shouldn't look like a slob. Get your shorts and your trainers on and get out running. You've got potential, pal, but you're nowhere near ready for us yet."

I walked out of the door and looked through the leaflets while Steve had a chat with the sergeant.

The blokes in the pictures appeared healthy, fit...and white.

There were no faces like mine in these photos. I might be the fittest lad in camp, but if I was getting shit from racists all the time, what would that be like? Could I handle it, just for the sake of being in the army?

Steve came out of the office. "Well, what do you reckon?" he said.

I held up the leaflets. "All these blokes...I dunno if I could match up to them. I don't want to feel like a failure. I just want to fit in and have a good life. I'm not sure this is for me, mate."

Steve grabbed my shoulder. "Like you said in there, you won't know until you give it a go. So just fucking give it a go. You've nowt to lose. And even if you don't make it, you won't be a fat little git anymore. I'll make sure of that. I've got some leave coming up soon. We'll go training, right? I'll beast the fuck out of you. Then you can decide. Deal?"

I smiled. "Deal."

"In the meantime, take the fella's advice, get off your arse and get running," Steve said.

I jumped on the bus back home. I felt that a lifeline was being dangled my way and if I grabbed it, I wouldn't regret it. I thought back to the moment I escaped from the madrassa and how my mate there, Abad, encouraged me over that wall... *"Either do it now or stay here...you've got more guts than you think...there's something about you, Mo...you're a survivor."*

I could hardly believe I'd done it – up and over the madrassa wall, followed by a dangerous trek through the north-west Frontier and back to the village I'd been billeted in before I was kidnapped and taken away. I was just a kid then, but I'd done it against the odds.

I think my determination had even impressed the family who'd sent me to the godawful hellhole in the first place.

Yeah, I had more guts than I thought, and my main focus from this moment on would be to get rid of the big one that hung over my jeans.

I scraped enough money together to buy a few bits of piece of sportswear from a charity shop, plus a cheap pair of trainers from a discount store, and with determination and a newfound energy I began to run. At first this was painfully embarrassing. I could barely manage a mile without feeling I needed life-support and I watched in shame as joggers twice my age and more passed me effortlessly on the canal with a cheery, 'Good morning!".

Gradually, though, I improved. Not by a lot – I hadn't quite realised how much damage I'd done to myself in a relatively short space of time – but the more I ran the fitter I became and I replaced the high I got from drink and drugs with the natural chemicals released into the brain via exercise.

The druggie mates I'd picked up over the past few months couldn't believe this leaner, fitter Mo. At first they took the piss, expecting me to cave in and rejoin them for sniffing sessions in doss houses or by old railway lines. When I didn't, they asked me outright what I was up to. So I told them – and immediately the laddish piss-taking turned into something much more sinister:

"What? You're joining the British Army? Infidels…"

"They're kuffars, man. Does that mean you're a kuffar now?"

"If you wanna join an army, join the mujahideen…"

"Wait til this gets out around Hawesmill…"

I didn't care what they said about me personally, but that last comment worried me. If the family found out I was hoping to join the British Army I feared they'd make my life hell. Rafiq would be on my case day and night.

It would go against everything those people believed in, and if they weren't already mortally ashamed of who I was and what I was, this would put the tin hat on it – quite literally.

I tried to push such thoughts away as I carried on training, pounding the canal towpath for a mile, two miles, three miles, four miles – until, finally, I made the magic five miles without collapsing. And by now I was well on the way to losing the spare tyre that the recruiting sergeant had kindly pointed out to me. When Steve arrived home on leave and saw me, he was obviously impressed.

"Fair play to you, Mo, you've carried out orders," he said. "That's a good sign. You'll need to do that without question if you join up. So…are you ready for a bit of real training?"

My God, did that guy beast me over the next week or so! As well as running miles every day he had me doing constant press-ups, star jumps, sit-ups, pull-ups and lifting weights. After every session I crawled back into my bed, exhausted but knowing that every bit of this pain was taking me a step closer to the dream I desperately wanted to make a reality. In my mind's eye I saw myself in uniform, marching proudly alongside my fellow soldiers having put my past far behind me. I hoped it was not an impossible dream. And everything hinged on my next conversation at the Army Careers Office.

After ten days of training and exercise the like of which I'd never experienced,

Steve considered I was ready for my next meeting with the recruiting sergeant. Again he arranged to meet me outside the office in Blackburn and I climbed aboard the bus full of excitement, anticipation and fear. Excitement and anticipation that a new phase of my life could be about to begin, and fear that I might not make the grade.

Apart from finding my mother, I'd never wanted something so much in my whole life as to become a soldier and the thought of failure weighed heavily on me.

"We're back, mate," Steve said to the recruiting sergeant. "What d'you reckon? Have I done a good job on him?"

Just like last time the sergeant appraised me and smiled. "You're looking good, lad," he said, "a lot sharper and leaner than when you came in here last time. Top effort."

"Think you can do owt with him?" Steve said.

"I'd say he stands a much better chance now than he did a month ago, mate."

The sergeant turned to me. "Have you thought any more about it then? What you'd like to do in the army?"

To be honest, I hadn't given it much thought. I hadn't considered anything other than being a regular squaddie. That would suit me just fine.

"I dunno," I said. "I'm happy to do anything." I wracked my brains to think of something I thought might sound practical and useful.

"How about being, like, a driver or a chef or summat?"

The sergeant laughed. "Well, the army needs people to do those jobs," he said, "but I think a lad like you might find those a bit boring after a while. I reckon you're up for a challenge. Am I right?"

"Yeah, I reckon so," I replied.

"That would be, 'Yes, sergeant'," he said. "Let's get you into the right frame of mind of mind from the off."

"Yes, sergeant."

"That's better. Now…have you ever thought about parachuting?"

"What?! Sorry…pardon, sergeant?"

"Parachuting. Chucking yourself out of a plane at great height, hoping you won't die."

The answer was no, I'd never thought about parachuting. Not in my wildest dreams could I see myself jumping from a huge aircraft into a combat zone. Even so, I'd been in risky situations before and although I wasn't about to tell a total stranger of my time in Pakistan, given that experience I reckoned I had it in me to try anything.

"No, sergeant, I haven't thought about it at all," I said, "but I could give it a go."

The sergeant was pleased. He told me there were vacancies in something called '7th Parachute Regiment Royal Horse Artillery', (7 Para) which was an outfit that jumped out of planes with large calibre field guns. Once they landed they set up these guns and started shelling the enemy. That sounded interesting. Even better, no horses appeared to be involved.

"So if you're up for that," he said, "you'll be sent up to Scotland for a medical and fitness assessment. Pass that, and it's Pirbright for 14 weeks basic training. Get through that, it's Phase 2 Artillery training at Larkhill in Wiltshire.

And if you survive it, then you join your regiment in Aldershot and the preparation for 'P Company' begins.

It's the hardest training you'll do outside the SAS selection.

And if you get through *that,* you're a fucking better man than me, I can tell you."

Forbidden Soldier

The sergeant winked at Steve. My head was spinning with places I'd never heard of and training sessions that sounded nothing less than horrendous. What was I about to sign up for?

"OK, sergeant," I said, "put me down. What's the worst that can happen?"

"You're about to find out," he said, rooting in a drawer for a handful of forms.

A week or so later I was back in my crappy little flat when there was a knock at the door. I opened it, expecting to see Jamie. He'd started running too and we were training together in the run-up to my departure for Scotland. But instead, four heavily bearded Asian blokes in salwar kameez clothing stood there. Without bothering with introductions they shoved their way in, banging the door behind them. They smelled heavily of sweat, garlic and cigarettes. One of them grabbed my throat and rammed me against the wall. He leaned right into my face.

"We've heard about you, kuffar," he snarled. "We've been told you're joining the army, right?"

I couldn't speak or even move my head. I stared wildly at him as he gauged my eyes for a reaction.

"There's no point lying," he continued. "You've been spotted, training with infidels. Soldiers. We know what you're up to. You're a disgrace to your brothers. Do you understand, kuffar?"

I understood well enough. I'd been expecting this visit while hoping it would never happen, and that I'd be able to slip away from this hellhole forever. But I wasn't prepared for what came next.

"Joining the British Army is *haram* (forbidden) in this community," he said.

"It is an offence against Islam, and all true Muslims. If you join, we will hunt you down and kill you. You got that, bastard?"

The use of that final word gave me the clue I needed. These guys had been sent by Rafiq, no doubt about that. He wouldn't do it himself, knowing that by now I could give as good as I got, physically speaking. So he'd sent in the tough guys, the elders, the religious police.

The big man loosened his grip on my neck and slapped me around the face a couple of times, like a bullying father would do to a kid. I winced and ducked, trying to avoid further blows. The man pushed me onto the carpet and delivered a kick to the belly with his cheap shoes. It didn't hurt much; it was more humiliating than anything else. Besides, I'd had worse.

The four men left the house, not bothering even to close the door. Almost expecting or hoping that passers-by would see me curled up and realise that I'd been subjected to a bit of community rough justice. I slammed it to with my foot, stood up and dusted myself down. In the past I'd have laid low, kept my head down, said 'Yes sir, no sir' to blokes like these and done exactly what they ordered. Would they really hunt me down and kill me? I couldn't be sure, but I reasoned that if they did, I'd have a bit of military training by then and I could do them a fair amount of damage before they did me in.

More than that, I didn't give a fuck. What they didn't know was that I'd already been summoned to Scotland.

I'd been sent a rail ticket that would take me from here to Preston, then on to Edinburgh where I'd be picked up and taken to an army camp somewhere out in the wilds, to be assessed for medical fitness. My bag was already packed and waiting for me in my bedroom. Death threat or not, I was on my first step to becoming a soldier.

Not until we are lost do we begin to understand ourselves.
Henry David Thoreau

Forbidden Soldier

Chapter Four

Bollocking after Bollocking

Forbidden Soldier

June 17, 1996. With the few possessions I had in an old rucksack, I stood in front of the barbed-wire-topped gate at Pirbright Barracks, Surrey, and took a deep breath before reporting to the guardroom. That summer, thousands of kids my age were going wild to the sounds of Oasis, Blur, and all the rest of the Britpop bands. Me – I was about to join the army and put myself through 14 weeks of shouting, bawling, endless exercise, crap food, drilling, marching and more shouting.

As I've said, I wanted to do this more than anything else, but even at this stage I had doubts. This was a massive decision to make. I'd passed the basic medical in Scotland no problem and the path to becoming a professional soldier was now wide open. I'd come this far but even then, my natural lack of confidence was saying, 'This is going to be rough, turn around, go home, have an easy life.' I knew what an 'easy life' meant – sitting at home on the dole, boozing, doing drugs and getting shit from people all around me. No thanks.

"Khan," said the corporal standing by the gate, ticking off my name. "Glad you're here. Head towards that big building 100 yards up there. Another medical and general brush-up." He stared at my ponytail, which was halfway down my back.

"And if you don't make it through basic, Khan," he said, "at least you'll not go home looking like a girly dickhead. Off you go."

Having my head shaved was the first proper introduction to army life. In basic training your identity is more or less stripped away, leaving you like a blank canvas ready for the military to make its mark on you. They want you to take orders without question, to eat, sleep, wash and shit when they tell you to, and not before. The whole point of being a soldier is that you're part of a fighting unit. Forget being an individual – you're a rank and a number and that's it. All personality must be drilled out of you at this stage to make sure you're in the right mindset for the role. That's how it is, and that's what I had to look forward to for the next 14 weeks.

A whole bunch of us were crowded into a lecture theatre, where we received various talks about what to expect in the British Army. As I looked round I realised I was pretty much the only non-white in the room; certainly, I was the only Asian. I'd expected this, of course, but the reality was just a bit terrifying. I recalled the words of the recruiting sergeant and wondered if I really could handle constant racism. I figured that it would just be part of a test – a test of strength to prove I was capable of joining the greatest, proudest army in the world. Time would tell.

I was shaken out of my thoughts by the voice of the corporal who'd been giving us our introductory talk. "Right!" he shouted, "over to you now, gentlemen. When I point at you, you'll stand up, give us your name and tell us why you want to become a soldier. You've got a minute each."

With that, he pointed at some poor spotty lad in the front row who promptly stood up and addressed the corporal as 'sir', got a major bollocking and was then so nervous he stumbled his way through his reasons for joining up.

"Pathetic! Sit down. Next!"

On it went, and each time one poor lad stood up and was teased or sniggered at, a nagging feeling in the pit of my stomach seemed to grow and grow. Desperately I tried to rehearse something that would impress everyone and earn me a round of applause, but nothing would come.

"You! Up on your hind legs!"

I stood up with as much speed as I could muster.

"Name?"

"Mo Khan, corporal." A predictable round of 'ooohhhhs' and sniggers. Somewhere behind me the word 'Paki' was whispered. I blocked it out and tried to gather my thoughts as rapidly as I could.

"OK, Khan, what bring you here on this sunny June day?"

Many, if not most of the other lads had talked about getting a career, learning a trade, travelling abroad, doing their bit for Queen and Country, etc. My reason was simple, so I said it:

"I want to be a soldier, corporal. That's it."

"A man of few words, eh?" said the corporal. "Fortunately, Khan, you're in the right place for soldiering. Sit down. Next!"

After the talk we were marched to barracks. Twelve of us would be sharing a room. Twelve lads full of bad habits and nasty smells who would quickly learn how to iron clothes, fold them perfectly, make beds, scrub floors, clean washing areas until they were gleaming and stand to attention at 5.30am when absolutely everything was inspected to the nth degree. And we would learn the hard way – bollocking after bollocking after bollocking.

When we weren't being bollocked we were marching and drilling as if our lives depended on it, and even then we were being bollocked. The regime was relentless and when it came to exercise and fitness I was literally struggling to keep up.

I thought I'd nailed this along the canals of East Lancashire but back then, when I'd finished my five miles, I could go home, have a brew, put my feet up and watch the telly. Not a chance of that here. Day and night, we were constantly on the move and when we weren't I could hardly speak for exhaustion.

Not that I was doing much speaking. I'd decided from the off that I'd just put my head down and keep myself to myself. In the madrassa I'd been the focus of cruel and unwanted attention for being 'different', and I didn't fancy a repeat of that particular horror. Also, I found it difficult to integrate with white people. Apart from Helen and Jamie and his family I hadn't really known any and I had little understanding of how this part of society operated. Their habits, customs, likes, dislikes, conversation and unwritten rules of behaviour were alien to me.

And even at 20 I was among the older recruits, but I certainly wasn't the oldest. That honour went to a guy from Preston called Pete, who was 26 and had earned himself the nickname 'granddad'. Like me, that made him 'different' and so we had a kind of bond. We hung about together, eating our meals in the cookhouse and buddying up during training exercises and PT. He was a constant piss-taker and could mimic my East Lancashire Asian accent to deadly effect.

Whenever I did talk to the other lads, the topic of conversation often fell into what regiment we'd be joining if we passed basic.

Whenever I mentioned 7 Para, those in the know would give me a certain look, followed by variations of the following statement:

"But that means you gotta do P Company...fucking good luck to you, mate. Rather you than me."

Whenever I heard this, my heart sank just that little bit further. To get into anything paratrooper-related, this series of eight tests of physical and mental strength must be passed with 'Pegasus Company', or 'P Company/P Coy' for short. At the time this was based at Aldershot but was about to transfer to Catterick in North Yorkshire, where I would take it provided I passed basic training. P Company is legendary in the British Army for being one of the toughest military qualifications in the world, involving timed marches carrying equipment, boxing (known as 'milling'), steeplechasing, an assault course at 55ft above the ground and a log race. Pass it, and you fully deserve the coveted maroon beret. Fail, and you are returned to unit. Many would return and attempt selection again, and pass, but those who failed several times would transfer to another regiment.

To pass, you need to show extraordinary levels of fitness, determination and aggression. And just a few weeks into basic training, I was struggling. I was quiet, shy and lacking in self-confidence, and I was beginning to wonder whether I'd made a terrible mistake in even deciding to join the army, never mind trying to become part of its elite. From where I was standing, P Company looked a long, long way ahead and I wasn't sure I'd even make it to the end of basic training.

As the days went by this played on my mind to the point that I felt I had no choice but to quit. I felt miserable, lonely and I didn't want to embarrass myself any further. I made an appointment to see the commanding officer, a Captain Day, to tell him I wanted to leave.

"Leave already?" he said in surprise as I stood to attention in front of him. "Why?"

"Sir, I don't think I'm up to the standard required. I don't think I'll pass and I don't want to get to the end and be failed, sir. That's why I'd rather leave now, sir."

The captain looked at me closely. "I see a lot of lads like you, Khan," he said. "They turn up here all starry-eyed about being a soldier, then reality hits and they want out. And mostly, they're right. They were never cut out for it in the first place. So off they go. But you...I'm not sure about you."

"Sir?"

"You're doing alright, Khan. You're not the fittest and you're a bit backward in coming forward, but you're doing OK. I have no major concerns about you."

"Sir..."

"You need to be more confident in your abilities. I think you can do this, but you have to believe in yourself. That goes for anything in life, not just the army. Do you understand?"

"Yes, sir."

"Good. In that case, I think you should give this a few more weeks. You'll probably find that you settle in, settle down, and do well. If not, report back in four weeks and you can pack up your belongings and leave. A deal?"

"Yes, sir, thank you very much, sir."

And with that, I marched out of the captain's office hardly believing what I'd heard. I thought I was useless.

He seemed to think otherwise. Why did he want me to stay? Was it because I was Asian, and the army needed to tick boxes? Possibly...but back in those days, possibly not. Could he, in fact, see that I had potential? And if that were true, should I carry on?

The reality was that I'd nothing to lose. The only alternative to the army was to go back to Hawesmill, and that was no alternative at all. Rafiq would never leave me alone, and if he ever found out I'd quit he would take great delight in reminding me what a failure I was.

Well, fuck him. If for no other reason, I was suddenly determined to pass basic training just to rub his nose in it. Even if I didn't get through P Coy and couldn't join 7 Para, the British Army would find a use for me, which is more than he'd ever done. With newfound confidence and determination I got stuck into what was left of the training and, just as the captain predicted, started to find that not only did army life suit me, but that I was actually enjoying it. Every day I pushed myself harder and harder; in training, but also when we were off-duty and spending time together as new recruits. I still felt awkward about trying to fit in with the rest of the lads but I discovered that even if I tried a little bit, I'd get something back.

Weirdly, I also began to feel at home. 'Home...' – a strange word to use, given that I'd never had much experience of what we might call real home life, certainly not since Dad died and we'd been farmed out.

A home was what I always needed and here it was, amid all the shouting and bollocking and piss-taking. The army had become home and family. It hadn't given up on me – there was no way I was going to give up on it.

Halfway through the training we were allowed a weekend's leave. The other lads were talking about seeing relatives, girlfriends and friends. I didn't say much about where I was going. There would be no relatives waiting for me on the platform at Preston station.

I didn't want to doss down in my old flat, all alone, so I contacted Jamie and invited myself to stay with him for a night or two. I was so knackered on the Friday evening I couldn't do much more than crash out on the family's sofa.

On the Saturday Jamie and I went fishing on the canal and although we had a pleasant afternoon I kept thinking about Hawesmill.

Curiosity got the better of me, and as afternoon turned into evening I pulled my baseball cap low over my eyes and decided to have a stroll around the old place.

As I walked up and down those grimy streets I reflected on all the times I'd spent there – living with Dad and Jasmine, then being billeted with Fatima, Abida and Rafiq before being duped into going to Pakistan and the madrassa. And as I wandered, feeling all the sorrow, bitterness and hatred welling up in me, I wondered about Mum. Where was she? And what lay behind her disappearance? I'd never believed the 'died in a car crash' line. Far too convenient and besides, I could sense she was out there somewhere.

One day I'll find you, Mum, I thought, *and you'll be really proud of me. I know you will…*

Such imaginings had kept me going in the past, and they were just as strong as ever. In my mind's eye I pictured myself turning up at her home in full uniform, standing tall as she opened the door.

I saw her jaw drop as the truth of this young man's identity dawned on her.

After a moment's hesitation she took me in her arms, welcoming me for the long-lost son that I was.

I paused, snapping out of my dream state. On the street corner ahead of me was one of the guys who'd threatened me with death. He was having a cigarette with another bloke and my footsteps on this quiet street had alerted them. Strangers weren't welcome in Hawesmill, especially ones in disguise. Immediately I crossed the street, pulling the peak of the baseball cap low over my brow.

I could feel their eyes boring into me as I passed by, trying to appear as nonchalant as possible. Something was said in Pashto that I couldn't quite make out, and I wasn't going to hang around to hear more.

As soon as I turned the street corner I broke into a run, knowing full well that these two would never be able to catch me now.

Eight weeks later and I'd passed basic training with flying colours. The captain's pep talk – and, in a strange way, that visit to Hawesmill – had galvanised my determination to 'be the best', as they said in the army recruitment adverts. In my mind I'd achieved something very special, something that came out of a confidence I never knew I had.

The passing out parade was pure pomp and ceremony – lots of perfect parading accompanied by a full regimental band, and cheered on by relatives and friends who'd gathered for the occasion.

Naturally, there was no-one there for me and when everyone piled back to the NAAFI for well-earned food and drink, I slipped back to the accommodation block, packed my stuff and set off for a cheap hotel just outside of Blackburn.

In some ways I was sad not to have received the cheers and the backslapping that everyone else deservedly got. Even so, as I called a taxi from the guard to take me to the station I was bursting with pride that I could finally call myself a British soldier.

Life is either a daring adventure or nothing at all.
Helen Keller

Forbidden Soldier

Chapter Five

World of pain

Forbidden Soldier

For a week I mooched around my old home town, keeping fit and trying to avoid being recognised. I couldn't wait to continue my army career and, unlike almost everyone on leave, was counting off the days until I could return. So it was with a mixture of relief and anticipation that I entered Larkhill Barracks on the southern edge of Salisbury Plain, home of the Royal Artillery and the place I'd learn to operate the 105 mm light gun.

Without getting too technical, this field gun is one of the most versatile pieces of equipment in the British Army. It can be towed by a medium weight vehicle, carried around the battlefield, underslung by a Chinook helicopter or parachuted out of a C-130 Hercules. It can even be fitted with skis for snowy areas. It is used to provide artillery support for ground troops going into battle by firing a barrage of shells ahead of the advance. 7 Para's primary role is to provide this support to the Parachute Regiment. In the battlefield the guns are just behind the Paras and a small team of soldiers from our regiment are bedded in with them. When they need our support, fire missions are sent to us over the radio and the guns fire upon the target locations.

Those of us arriving at Larkhill that day needed to know every single inch of that weapon.

On exercise and on combat operations the gun crew has to work like a well-oiled machine.

Every second counts and men's lives depend on your efficiency and precision Day after day we learned how to operate the gun, how to keep it maintained, how to load it, aim it, fire it and transport it in a variety of ways. After a couple of weeks you felt you were married to this thing.

It was at Larkhill that I encountered my first bit of racism in the army. One of my fellow trainees was a Liverpool lad called Boz. Although I still couldn't quite get past my natural shyness I was making efforts in that direction and gradually I found they were paying off. I could banter with the lads more easily and I didn't feel as much of a loner anymore. Mainly, the blokes accepted me into their circle but my antenna for trouble always twitched when Boz was around. There was something about him I didn't quite trust...

One day we were in the gun park, a large hangar where all the artillery pieces were kept. As usual, we were being drilled on some aspect of the mechanics of the light gun when I accidentally dropped a large spanner, hitting the ground with a heavy 'clang!' and obviously triggered something in Boz.

"Oi, you fuckin' divvy!" he shouted. "Be fuckin' careful next time, will yer?!"

"Who are you calling a divvy?" I replied, turning to him and looking him right in the eye.

"You, dickhead," he said, pointing at my face and spitting out my name with all the venom he could muster. "I'm calling you a divvy, you dirty fuckin' Paki bastard. What're you gonna do about it then?!"

I didn't think twice. I socked him a right hook to the side of his face. I wasn't going to take any of that shit, especially not from him.

He retaliated immediately, clobbering me good and hard and grabbing on to the lapel of my combat jacket in a bid to give me a kick in the nuts.

I swung him round and within seconds we were on the floor, kicking, punching, wrestling and spitting like two cats in a bag. Our instructor and a couple of the lads pulled us apart and dragged us to our feet. Immediately we were sent back to block to cool off, and later we received an almighty bollocking from a bombardier. We could've easily been disciplined, with the possibility that we might both be dishonourably discharged. However, after an apology from Boz and an acknowledgement from me 'that these things sometimes happen' (which, of course, they shouldn't, and there is no excuse for racism of any sort. However, this was the army in the 1990s – it wasn't always the most enlightened, free-thinking institution on earth) we shook hands and agreed to forget about it. Which we did, and eventually became mates.

Once we'd passed all the tests and had carried out live firing exercises on Salisbury Plain it was time to finally join our regiments. Some of the blokes went off to 29 Commando, while I was headed to Aldershot and 7 Para.

By now, and having learned what I would be doing in 7 Para, the prospect of a career in the army was no longer daunting. I'd done better than I could ever have imagined when I was slumped in a chair in that doss-house, pissed, stoned and with zero purpose.

Finally, I'd woken up and although I'd had to leave almost every single aspect of my old life behind, that was hardly a loss.

I kept in touch with Jasmine, but as time passed she would become busy with her growing family and opportunities for anything more than an occasional phone call were pretty much non-existent.

The army held no terrors for me and I was prepared for what they were going to throw at me next – the dreaded 'P Company'.

I arrived at Aldershot with a new title – 'Gunner Khan' – and a readiness for the training I was about to undergo before P Company proper began.

On arrival I was placed into 'P Troop'. This is a unit within 7 Para which prepares you, by way of constant beastings and regular, strenuous exercise, for P Coy selection. If I thought basic training was hard, it was literally a walk in the park compared to this. Training to be a paratrooper is a hellish experience and we were beasted from the second we woke up to the minute we went to bed, in the most basic accommodation imaginable. And even then we were often woken up in the middle of the night for 30 minutes of sit-ups, squats, star jumps and burpees. The training was relentless and went on for a full two weeks with little or no respite. Gradually, there was a thinning out of the guys who'd volunteered for this madness until there was 4 nutcases left who were prepared to go all the way or die in the process.

I could've jacked this in at that moment and slipped into another regiment – the Royal Artillery, most likely – where I could've continued my army career quite happily, and without this world of pain.

But by now I was determined to get my maroon beret and parachute wings and become a fully-fledged paratrooper at any cost.

And I'd yet to jump out of an aeroplane! Sometimes I wondered whether I would go through all of this, just to discover that I had a chronic fear of heights and wouldn't be able to go through with the jump. I realised, though, that worrying about this would do me no good at all, and that I'd just have to face it when the time came.

Towards the end of the week a group of P Company training staff arrived at Aldershot from Infantry Training Centre in Catterick, North Yorkshire, to assess the fitness of those who wanted to attempt P Coy.

If you passed you were shipped to Catterick to start P Coy.

Anyone reading this who's ever endured the week-long P Company Test will know that it's the closest thing to hell on earth that you can possibly imagine, except for Special Forces selection. Most of the time you're wet, dirty and freezing. You're dragged across moors, up hills and through rivers wearing combat gear and carrying a 35lb 'bergen' army-issue rucksack. And if you're not carrying that, you're part of a team shouldering a 60-kilo telegraph pole over two miles of what the army politely describes as 'undulating terrain'; in truth, a nasty, smelly, dark and dank bog, plus hills that feel like mountains.

Then you're sent on to the 'trainasium', an aerial assault course, balancing like a tightrope walker on tree-top ladders and bars at 55ft above the ground.

If you haven't fainted from fear and exhaustion by then, you're running all over the place in a bid to beat the clock, or punching the shit out of someone you'd otherwise call a mate in the spirit of 'milling'.

Any weakness, hesitation or failure to complete each challenge in the allotted time means you're automatically binned, and you return to your regiment with your tail firmly between your legs. That week, I saw grown men freeze with fear on the trainasium and others cry in shame as they completed a gruelling run, only to find they were just a vital few seconds late. By this stage I thought I was super-fit but being short and naturally stocky I struggled, especially on the individual timed runs carrying weight, and on several occasions just narrowly squeaked in ahead of the clock.

I was given the number '68', which was painted on my helmet, top and trousers. For an entire week, all I could hear was "Come on, 68, you lazy fucker, get a move on, get a move on, you useless piece of shit, think you're gonna be an Airborne soldier, not a fuckin' chance!!!" Etc etc, until I tuned out of the perma-bollockings and went into a state of tunnel vision, literally just focusing on the next step. By the end of the week I knew I'd done OK in terms of passing everything within time. But had I shown sufficient determination and fighting spirit? That was the one thing I couldn't be certain of. I'd toughened up hugely since joining the army but inside I was still a shy kid, awkward in social situations and unsure about the ways of white people. None of that disqualified me from being a soldier but I was aware I wasn't quite 'one of the lads', and in the army being part of a team is everything.

The day of judgement came all too quickly. Still exhausted from our efforts, the survivors of P Company were marshalled into a lecture hall at the camp and ordered to sit down.

There, a sergeant read a list of numbers and after each one shouted 'Pass!' or 'Fail!' Just like my first day at Pirbright, my stomach lurched all over the place as I waited my turn.

"Number 68!"

"Sir!" I stood up, ramrod-straight. If I'd failed, I was determined to walk out of there with as much dignity as I could muster.

"Pass!"

The goosebumps ran right up my spine and down my arms. Had I heard right? I could barely believe it. Less than a decade previously I'd been shut up in a madrassa on the Pakistan/Afghanistan border, not knowing if I would survive such a cruel experience.

In a white man's world, something like passing P Company is no mean achievement, but for someone of mixed race and an Asian upbringing...well, to say I was proud of myself is an understatement. I was dying to cheer, or even crack a smile, but then I saw the devastated expressions on the lads who'd failed and, as ever, I decided to keep myself to myself.

Now it was back to Aldershot for a few days before heading north to Oxfordshire and RAF Brize Norton for the final part of my induction into 7 Para. Although I'd come this far I still hadn't earned my 'wings' – the sew-on badge you get to wear when you pass the parachuting part of the course. As a newbie you're the lowest of the low and you don't earn any respect until you've done that thing and leapt from an aircraft.

We spent a week jumping off structures of increasing height, practising how to land, how to roll, how not to smash your ankles to pieces and how to remember to open your parachute.

All this took place in a large hangar but all the time you know that somewhere on this airfield there is an RAF Hercules transport plane waiting with your name on it.

Finally that day came. Like the rest of the lads I was nervous but tried not to show it. We'd all passed P Company, of course, but no matter how hard that is, it isn't likely to kill you. Parachuting is a dangerous occupation and although the chances of something going wrong are slim, when they do you can end up badly injured or, more likely, dead. As I boarded the aircraft in a state of excited anticipation I thought back to the day at the army recruitment centre when the sergeant asked me how I fancied jumping out of an aircraft. I'd gone along with it, never imagining I'd get this far. *A chef or maybe a driver*...that's what I'd asked for, but here I was, having made it all the way. Almost.

The aircraft climbed to around 900 feet. We would be static line jumping; clipping the parachute ripcord to a rail above the Herc's doorway, flinging ourselves out one by one and hoping the parachute opened. At the signal we got up and shuffled towards the door, completing final checks on the way. The door opened, the green light blinked and the first man jumped without hesitation. Ahead of me, I could see a few of the lads taking a deep breath before they did it, but they did it nonetheless and needed no pushing.

Now it was my turn. Below, I could see the ground moving slowly past. *This is it*, I thought. *Sod it...*

Out I went, one thousand, two thousand, three thousand, check canopy – the ground rushing up to meet me until

I felt a violent tug on my shoulders and the sensation of being yanked upwards back towards the aircraft.

For a moment I just hung there, relieved that the canopy had opened. Then I remember...checks. There were certain checks to be made before I hit the ground and because of the low altitude we'd jumped at, that would be seconds rather than minutes. I did my checks and pulled on the parachute harness to see if I could steer the thing. It seemed to work and, remembering what I'd learned in drill.

You never really quite get over the shock of coming to earth with a bang, but at least I didn't break my legs. "Nice one, Khan," said the ground staff, "unclip your harness, fold up your canopy double quick and join the rest."

We assembled in the field we'd landed, buzzing with excitement and grinning like idiots. Like the rest of us, I just wanted to do it again and again. Back at hanger we were handed our 'wings'.

Finally, after all that, I was a trained paratrooper ready to join 7 Para and do the job I'd signed on for all those months ago.

That evening, the rest of the lads went for an almighty piss-up to celebrate. I forced myself to be sociable and joined them for an hour, but when the songs started and beer was flying everywhere I beat a quiet retreat and went back to my room. Despite everything I'd been through, I still had difficulties with majority society, even down to ordering pints and when to get a round in. I just didn't get it, and often it was easier just to make myself scarce. Largely, the lads understood it but as ever, I didn't quite fit in.

All the wonders you seek are within yourself.
Thomas Browne

Chapter Six

Prisoner of war

Forbidden Soldier

It took a crew of six to manhandle the 105mm gun that would be our constant companion wherever we went. I can imagine what it must have been like in the days when the army used horses, spending every day caring for something in the hope that when the crunch came and battle commenced, it wouldn't let you down. The crew – a sergeant or a bombardier in charge, a lance-bombardier second-in-command and the rest of us gunners, would spend most of the day working on the weapon to keep it in good order before training on it when we had the opportunity.

To fire the 105mm you first input the coordinates of your target, making sure the barrel is facing the right way (always a good start!). Closest to the gun are the loader and the rammer. The loader places the shell inside the gun's breech, making sure that the copper band around the base of the shell has secured it in place. The rammer then uses a rod with a rubber grommet top to shove the shell down the barrel of the gun until it reaches the rifling. Next, the loader places a cartridge shell into the barrel, the rammer closes the breech and the gun is ready to fire. In the meantime the rest of us are getting the next rounds of ammunition ready, listening to the radio for orders and recalibrating the gunsights if necessary.

The gun is fired, the recoil comes back and immediately the breech has to be opened to let the cartridge shell fall out. While the gun is being reloaded the commander is on the radio, receiving information from the command post.

The type of shell might need to be changed depending on the target, for example to a high-explosive type. The new orders will be shouted out to the crew who will do their thing while the commander receives information about bearing elevation. When this is received the barrel will be elevated and the target coordinates set. Once everything is done the command post is radioed to let them know we're ready. Then as soon as the command comes, we fire again.

After a couple of months I could repeat this routine in my sleep and even now, years later, I can still recall exactly how this gun is operated. In the army you learn to do something and you repeat it over and again until it becomes second nature. You don't need to think, you just do it. That's what being a soldier is about, of course. Not thinking, just carrying out orders. Which isn't too bad in peacetime, but when you're under fire or you're firing on someone else knowing you're probably killing them, well... more of that later.

We also had to learn to jump out of a Hercules aircraft with our pet gun and its Pinzgauer towing vehicle and have the thing set up and ready to fire within minutes of landing. Getting everyone, plus gun, tow-truck and related equipment, on board the Herc is a feat of logistics itself. The gun and vehicle have to be secured inside the aircraft and the parachutes fitted, then the ammunition is wheeled on in huge cases.

The aircraft takes off, climbs to the correct height, the drop zone is reached, the tailgate drops open and the gun goes out, supported by three parachutes.

Next is the vehicle, followed by the ammo. The Herc does a circle, the crew piles out one at a time, we secure the ground, reach the vehicles and get everything stripped down and ready for action.

One of the perks of army life is being able to train in unusual locations across the world, visiting places that the average squaddie like me might otherwise never have seen.

Of course, these aren't holidays by any stretch of the imagination but there is a fraction of spare time in which to do a bit of sightseeing or just hang out with the locals.

So a few months after receiving my beret wings, we received orders that we were going on a six-week training exercise to Alberta, Canada. I was very excited but also anxious at the same time. Apart from Pakistan and Afghanistan I'd never been out of the UK and although I'd heard great things about Canada, leaving the familiarity of Britain was initially nerve-wracking. We were heading for the British Army Training Unit Suffield (BATUS), located on the Canadian prairies and, within an area the size of Dorset, the British Army's biggest training facility.

The guns were sent ahead of us by sea and two weeks later we were due to fly out after them.

Our orders were to parade at the barracks at 02:30hrs on the morning of the flight. A few of the lads decided to go into London on the piss and although I was still unfamiliar with British pub culture I tagged along, hoping to learn something and, as ever, just wanting to fit in. We caught the train around 14:30hrs from Aldershot to Euston and went to a few bars, and before we knew it, we were all hammered.

"Excuse me, sir...sir, excuse me please..."

I felt a hand push against my shoulder and awoke to find it was attached to a uniformed arm.

Luckily for me, it wasn't a khaki-wearing figure of authority waking me up but a railway guard.

"Excuse me, sir...I thought I should let you know that the train is terminating here. You'll need to get off."

I was completely disorientated and the hangover hadn't even begun. I was still hopelessly drunk, but somehow managed to pull myself out of the seat and onto the platform.

I looked around, hoping to see one of the lads also falling out of the carriage and on to the platform. But there was no-one else around and the station itself seemed worryingly unfamiliar. Then I read the sign on the platform: Southampton Central.

Shit! Those bastards must've got off at Aldershot and, for a laugh, left me flat out in the carriage. It was now around midnight and I had just two hours to report for duty, my kit all packed and ready and, more importantly, in a state of complete sobriety. I asked a guard if there was a train going back to Aldershot.

"I'm afraid not," came the reply. "The first train goes out at 6:20. Sorry..."

Not as sorry as I'd be when my troop commander at camp found out I was AWOL. Panicking, I found a phone box and with a deep breath called the guardroom at the barracks. The guard commander answered and, knowing he wouldn't want to be bullshitted at this time of the day (or at any time of the day, to be honest).

"Right, Khan," he said once I'd stopped wittering on, "here's what you're going to do.

There will be a taxi rank outside the station.

Get a cab now, tell them you want taking to Aldershot ASAP and don't take 'no' for an answer. Got that?"

"Bombardier, but...I don't have any money."

The five seconds or so of silence were among the most painful I'd ever endured.

"I see," he said. "In that case, find a cab driver, tell him what's happened and bring him to the phone."

I did as I was ordered, only to be told to 'piss off' by a couple of cabbies who thought I was barking mad.

Finally I found a guy willing to listen and escorted him to the phone box. After a brief conversation, the cabbie replaced the receiver. "OK," he said, "we're leaving. Fasten your seatbelt, cos I've been told not to hang about."

Just under an hour later we arrived at the camp. As the taxi driver was paid handsomely for his mission of mercy I received an almighty bollocking from the officer on duty, who promised faithfully that this would be reported to my troop commander straight away. With his threats ringing in my ears I ran full pelt to the block, put on my uniform, grabbed my bergen and headed to the parade ground where all the departing troops were gathered. I approached my battery sergeant major and asked to 'fall in', i.e. get on parade.

He turned to me, and if I thought I'd already had one huge bollocking, nothing could've prepared me for what I was about to receive. I was called every name under the sun, in front of the whole battery, and as I stood there and took it meekly, I could feel my whole face reddening – an unusual reaction inherited from the European side of the family which always caused amusement.

And not least now, as the lads I'd been out with, looking fresh as daisies, could barely contain their laughter.

After the bawling-out was over and I fell in I felt very low, just like I did when Rafiq wore me down with the nasty asides and sneering jibes.

But I was a boy then: now I was a soldier in the British Army. I needed to man up and quickly, and I did.

For the next six weeks we roughed it on the Canadian prairie, training to operating the guns in all conditions, day and night.

We moved from position to position constantly, firing shell after shell, all the time improving our skills.

And whenever there was a need for someone to do a shitty job, I'd be that person – the punishment for arriving on parade pissed and late. From guard duty, cleaning out latrines for officers when out in the field, polishing equipment, etc., and all without complaint.

By now I'd been in the army for a few years and since Canada we'd done plenty of training exercises in the UK and Scotland, along with military parachuting. The good news for me was that I'd been put forward for a promotional course to receive my first stripe and become a lance bombardier. This was a four-week management course involving aspects including leadership and confidence training.

The latter included a session during which you had to stand up and talk about a subject for two minutes. I was dreading this and when my name was called I could feel my stomach lurch to the bottom of my boots.

"Gunner Khan," the staff trainer said, "you have two minutes to talk about this. " And he handed me a toothbrush.

When you're talking about things like toothbrushes, two minutes is a very, very long time.

"This is a toothbrush," I said, to muffled sniggers, "most people use them twice a day, morning and night, though others use them after meals too. They come in different colours and size, and the bristles are different if you're a kid, or have tooth problems..."

On and on I went, wondering when this torture would stop. At 90 seconds I began to dry up but when I paused for a second or two I could see the staff trainer's eyes on me. I waffled on for a bit longer until he gave me the signal to stop and I sat down, feeling a prat for talking about toothbrushes but also secretly pleased that I'd made it through. By now, my confidence was really growing.

Soon after we were deployed on another six-week training exercise, this time to Jordan and working alongside the Jordanian army. As usual the guns were sent by sea while we arrived at King Hussein International Airport and were taken to an army base. We were briefed on the political situation in the country and any potential threats from nearby countries. While the rest of the troops were preparing the guns and equipment ready for training, those on the leadership course would complete the last two weeks of it here, so we were separated from the rest and carried on with our training.

Towards the end of the course seven of us were in the back of a truck heading to a training area, where we would be dropped off and with maps and compasses. We would tab (march) to the top of a hill and observe an enemy position, the 'enemy' being other soldiers from our regiment. We were to gather as much intel as possible, head back to the pickup location and make our way to camp.

Those were the orders – or at least we thought they were. Suddenly there was panic from the front of the cab and our vehicle came to a violent stop.

In front of us was a makeshift checkpoint manned by heavily armed men, pickup trucks blocking the dirt track.

Our vehicle was surrounded by this collection of unidentified troops, wearing a mixture of military and traditional Arab clothing and screaming for us to get out of the truck. We were all carrying weapons but as is usual on exercises like this we only packed blank ammunition. Without hesitation the Arab soldiers dragged us to the ground, taking our equipment, weapons and maps before zip-tying our hands and removing our boot laces. Empty sandbags were then forced over our heads amid constant screaming and shouting.

Having a smattering of Arabic picked up from my days in the madrassa, I listened carefully to what was being said. I couldn't quite follow the conversations but something about it just didn't feel right. The words used seemed inappropriate to what was happening, and the pronunciation was wrong in some parts. We were dragged into the back of the pickup trucks and after an extremely bumpy, unnerving ride we were hauled out of the vehicles and thrown into a darkened room. The door was slammed shut.

We hardly dared speak for fear of alerting our captors to the fact we were scared. And we were scared, and shocked too. We'd been led to believe that Jordan was a safe country and now this – capture by people we assumed were terrorists. The shouting in Arabic continued outside but again, the words used did not sound right to me. It seemed that our captors weren't terrorists at all, and that we'd been 'kidnapped' by our own training staff as part of the course.

Even so, we were treated like prisoners of war, and possibly worse than that. We were placed in stress positions around the room while white noise was blasted from an old radio in the background.

Still hooded, we received punches and kicks to different parts of our bodies and cold water poured down our backs. This continued for what seemed hours and while we knew it was a game, it was one being played for real. We just had to get though it – which we did – but one of our guys broke down, and started kicking off. Even though it was just part of the training he completely lost it. Not good when you're under intense pressure.

The course came to an end and for the remainder of the time in Jordan we joined our unit and continued with our live firing and training with the Jordanian army. Six weeks later we were back in Aldershot and, with no small amount of pride, I received my first stripe. I was now a lance bombardier.

Change the problem by changing your mind.
Ken MacLeod

Chapter Seven

Profile of an Islamic terrorist

Forbidden Soldier

As the end of my minimum four-year signing on period with the army approached, I began to wonder whether I wanted to stay in for much longer. The job was great but very repetitive, and a certain level of boredom was creeping in. There comes a point in every soldier's career when he, (and back then it was pretty much all 'he') wants to put all their training to use in a real combat situation. Personally, I wasn't looking for a fight but would've willingly taken part in one had the opportunity arisen. As it was, the very end of the 1990s was a peaceful time for the British Army. Northern Ireland was over, the Balkans conflict hadn't sucked us in and the horrific events of 9/11 which led to such trauma around the world were a few years away yet.

We continued to train and train but increasingly I wondered what the point of it all was. I'd proved myself to be a capable soldier and, despite the odds and my Muslim background, had been accepted as one of the lads. There was still the occasional comment or sideways glance but I'd long since learned to deal with that. I liked being part of the gang, even if I still felt I didn't quite fit in, and the army had become my family. I was just keen to find another challenge in life, either in or out of the army.

Officers are trained to notice when one of the soldiers under their command isn't quite cutting it and one afternoon I was called in to see my troop captain.

He was polite and friendly, asking me if I was OK and whether I was experiencing any difficulties.

"You seem a bit detached, Khan," he said. "You know how it is when you're in a close-knit team. If one of the blokes isn't quite right, everyone feels it."

"Sorry, sir," I replied.

"It's not a case of 'sorry', Khan," he replied. "You're a good soldier. But something's chewing at you and I'm not the only one to notice. So come on…spit it out."

I told him that while I liked the life and the blokes, I was looking for something else. Another challenge, maybe, and perhaps outside of the army.

"We don't want to lose you, Khan," the captain said. "What can I do to make you stay?"

A pay rise, maybe, I thought, but didn't say. The answer would've been a definite 'no!'

I shrugged. "Sir, I don't know, sir…"

The captain mentioned he'd seen me skydiving in Canada and had I enjoyed that? I replied in the affirmative. We'd done a little of it out there on days off and I'd found it exhilarating. But for me, it was just for fun.

"In that case," he said, "would you be interested in joining the Royal Artillery parachute display team?"

The question reminded me of the time at the recruiting office in Blackburn, where I'd been asked if I fancied jumping out of planes.

"Sir, I haven't thought about it," I said, "But sure, I'd give it a go."

"OK, Khan," he replied, "have a think about it, let me know and I'll see what I can do."

"Sir, I'm up for it."

Within weeks I was off to Netheravon, Wiltshire, for selection. There were six of us, all from different units within the Royal Artillery. We had to complete ten static line jumps; no problem for me, but a test for others who'd never previously jumped. Following this, we had to complete three freefall jumps from 3,000 feet, during which you were solely responsible for pulling the ripcord which deploys the parachute. If successful and selected, there were three places we could be sent as an assistant skydiving instructor, learning to skydive, assist the instructor and help run the skydiving centre. These were located in Cyprus, Germany or Netheravon. For some reason a senior NCO at the Netheravon drop zone did not like me and another soldier – who happened to be black – and had us both sent to Germany.

I was posted to an army parachute training centre in Paderborn. This would be an 18-month-long position, during which I'd help to run a joint services parachute centre sky-diving school which, in addition to training soldiers, also instructed civilians. There was a bit of extra money involved and I found I enjoyed teaching civilians to overcome their worst fears and leap out of a plane. This was a happy time for me; somehow, I fitted in at Paderborn in a way I'd never felt possible back in the UK and I'd go out pubbing and clubbing with my fellow instructors who always treated me as an equal. Being skydivers held a certain amount of kudos both with the local girls and British women living on or near the base, and we had a lot of fun together.

When the weather wasn't great in Germany, usually over the winter, we'd be sent to train abroad, which for me meant two trips to California. On my first visit to America I was stopped by border control at Los Angeles International Airport and escorted to a room.

Now, this was a year or so before 9/11 but there had been Islamic terror attacks on the United States and its allies, in particular two US embassy bombings in Kenya and Tanzania. So US Immigration was on the lookout for anyone who might be planning to bring the fight direct to American soil and unfortunately my face fitted the general profile of an Islamic terrorist, in that I was brown and had a funny-sounding name.

I was ordered to take a seat in the room and wait until I was called. As I looked around, I noticed all my fellow interviewees were either black or brown. The sullen silence in the room was broken only by a uniformed security official calling out a name and taking the passenger away for questioning. I began to worry about what they might say when they discovered I'd spent time in Pakistan. Would they know I was brainwashed in a madrassa by supporters of the Taliban, the very organisation who, at this moment, were taking Afghanistan back to medieval times with their cruel and brutal form of religious-inspired justice? If they did, I swore I'd look them right in the eye and tell them I was a British soldier on a training exercise. Luckily for me, my commanding officer arrived with a letter explaining who I was, and I was sprung before any questioning could take place.

When I caught up with the others I was the butt of the jokes, of course.

"Were you hiding a bomb or summat, Khan?" "Have you got uncles in the Taliban?" "Are you a spy?" All that kind of thing, meant in jest and taken in the same spirit. Even so, their jibes hurt a bit, emphasising as always that I was somehow 'different'.

Back in Germany we carried on with team training and manning the skydiving centre.

One afternoon I was assisting with a group of civilian jumpers when I started talking to a British woman about the same age as me. She told me her name was Jessica and we chatted about this and that before boarding the plane. As she was being strapped to her instructor in readiness to complete a tandem skydive she told me she had a manager's job in a shop and was married to a serving soldier. I have to confess that I was somewhat disappointed to hear the latter piece of information because there was something about this girl I really liked. She had a confidence about her that drew me in – plus she was funny and beautiful. I checked her harness and although conversation was all but impossible within the confines of a small, noisy light aircraft we smiled at each other on the journey to the drop zone.

Jessica and her instructor went out first, closely followed by me recording the whole jump. As we floated towards earth I could see Jessica's cheeks flapping in the wind, which really made me laugh. She smiled, wondering what was tickling me, and I gave her a wave. Back on the ground I told her what had caused my amusement.

"Oi!" she shouted, mock-seriously, "that's not funny!" She smiled again, and I knew I was smitten. I also knew that there was very little I could do about it. She was a married woman, and that was that.

By now it was late summer 2001 and apart from my aching heart, life was good. The weather was beautiful then, giving us plenty opportunities to practise our freefall routines and have a laugh with the civilians we jumped with. One afternoon, after another successful skydive, we went into a local café for a drink. We'd visited this place many times before and it was always a hive of activity and noise, with off-duty soldiers and their families mixing with German civilians.

Today, however, you could've heard a pin drop as we opened the door and walked in. "Was it something we said?" joked one of the lads. "*Vier bier bitte,*" asked another of our party in his best worse German. But instead of smiling and starting to pour his order, the German barmaid hushed him to be quiet and pointed at the TV on the wall.

The crowded bar was silently watching the images that were being repeated over and over, of a plane hitting a skyscraper full-on. At first I thought they were glued to a disaster movie. But after a few seconds I realised this was not fiction. Something terrible was happening, something I felt even at that moment would change the course of history.

"What the fuck's going on?" whispered one of our lads to an off-duty squaddie, his short hair and tattoos making him easily recognisable from the Germans gathered around him.

"Terrorist attack, innit?" he replied. "Twin Towers in New York. They reckon it's Arabs."

We watched in horror as what looked like a civilian airliner hit the building. The pictures were shown again and again, and the screams on the ground in Manhattan could clearly be heard over the running commentary.

It looked like the world was ending. Next second, the viewpoint shifted and it seemed that another plane had hit the second tower. This time, the screams weren't confined to the streets of New York. The café erupted in shock as the drama unfolded, and the cries for revenge by the British squaddies watching this happening live were as ugly as they were determined.

In the corner of my eye I could see a few looks cast my way and occasional mutterings of 'Paki bastards' 'fucking Muslims', 'terrorist twats'.

All that and more, and in the days which followed I'd get ribbed by the lads, who started calling me 'Osama'. Now, I'd been in the army long enough not to give too much of a shit, even when they were joking that they were 'glad the planes are locked in the hangar' when I was around. I'd learned to take it all as banter, but in the days immediately after 9/11 it was hard not to be stung by their words. We learned that we were to be deployed back to England within days, no doubt to prepare for something pretty bloody huge on the horizon for all of us in the armed forces.

Before we left for England we had a long series of nights out, most of which I tagged along to. It was during one of these that I ran into Jessica. We spent the whole night chatting and agreed to meet the following night. As I've mentioned at the time Jessica was married to a serving soldier.

But the relationship was falling apart and they were in the process of splitting up. Jessica told me all about it and as I listened we both knew we had established an unspoken bond.

Then I told her my story – a story I'd told very, very few people at that stage – and now it was her turn to listen, open-mouthed, as I described my life in Lancashire with the family, my forced exile to Pakistan and the time I spent in the madrassa.

That night we bared our souls and agreed to see each other again. In short, we'd clicked and by our third or fourth date we were a couple. Jessica's family lived on the south coast, not too far away from my regiment's HQ in Aldershot, and she planned to return to that area following her separation. At this stage we agreed to take things slowly but deep down we both knew it wouldn't be long before we would be together.

While some sections of 7 Para went to Afghanistan under the banner of Operation Herrick to pursue the war on the Taliban, I was continuing my training and regular parachuting displays.

The Royal Artillery's parachute display team were named the Black Knights. These are the kind of guys you'll see at military-themed public events or large arena show, jumping out of planes from thousands of feet up, maybe releasing canisters of coloured smoke, and landing in very tight formation. Having had extensive parachute training I was in no fear of the task. However, there was a selection process and I was up against many other good parachutists so I had to be up to the mark.

To qualify for the team you had to have a certain amounts of jumps and training, which included packing your own parachute, and jumping with huge flags and smoke canisters strapped to your ankles. Much of the focus was on landing in a small area, taking into account wind speed and the direction of wind to land safely and accurately.

You also had to be adaptable, mastering jumping from 13,000 feet or as low as 3,000 feet, making this look effortless in front of thousands of spectators. And at the end of the display jump, you'd be required to gather in your area of the festival or event, pack the parachutes and talk to members of the public interested in what you did, or who were keen to join the army themselves.

After passing the course I was ready for my first display jump. I was dispatched to the Royal Artillery Barracks at Woolwich, London, where the Black Knights were based.

My first display was at the barracks on Armed Forces Day. There were six of us jumping, and four members on the ground, in a small fenced-off area, with spectators all gathered around.

A large T-shaped object was placed on the ground in the centre of the arena which would be our target landing spot. We took off in a Cessna aircraft from a nearby airport. That day, the cloud base was low and we were jumping from 3,000ft. This is a low jump and if something should go wrong, for example the parachute not opening properly, you only have a very short amount of time to deal with it by cutting away the parachute (by pulling two cords on your harness in the correct order to release the bad chute) deploying your reserve chute and then try to steer and land in a safe place.

We exited the plane above the barracks and I deployed the chute straight away. After a few safety checks, I turned the chute towards the landing area, reached into a pouch strapped around my waist and lowered the Union Jack flag.

The huge piece of material was dangling below me as I started to fly the canopy towards the landing area.

As I got closer to the ground, I could hear the ground crew giving commentary over large speakers…"and next, ladies and gentlemen, we have Lance Bombardier Khan, who has made over 300 jumps and is serving with 7th Parachute Regiment RHA." As I landed next to the T-shape material, I collapsed the chute and saw children and parents all clapping and waving. We then made our way to our tent to talk to those interested about the jump we'd just made.

I really enjoyed the experience, and even the discussions with the adults and kids who'd come to chat with us.

By the end of 2002 we all pretty much knew that something was looming on the horizon. American President George W. Bush was making louder and louder noises about Iraq being a terrorist state and seemed determined to finish the job his father had started back in 1991.

More importantly, UK Prime Minister Tony Blair was ready to stand 'shoulder to shoulder' with Bush, meaning only one thing – that at some stage we would be going to war. I was now facing the reality. I just hoped I wouldn't be exiting 7 Para in a body bag.

Strength is what we gain from the madness we survive.
Unknown

Forbidden Soldier

Chapter Eight

All guns – FIRE

Forbidden Soldier

Somewhere on the Kuwait/Iraq border, March 19, 2003.

You could've cut the atmosphere with a knife, or a bayonet. Crouched in my shellscrape, awaiting the order that would begin this all-out assault on Iraq, I glanced at the lads around me. Some were asleep, or what passed for sleep on this most tense, testing of nights. Others were like me; awake, alert and wondering if they would see another dawn.

We had no idea what to expect once battle started. The Iraqis weren't the best-trained army in the world, but there were a lot of them. And, according to the governments who'd sent us here, they were equipped with 'weapons of mass destruction', which we took to mean poison gas, and the reason we were all wearing NBC ('nuclear, biological and chemical') suits.

It was getting dark, the kind of clear, cool starlit evening that you only experience in desert places. It reminded me of my grandmother's house in Northwest Pakistan. As a boy I sat in her compound, trying to count the countless millions of stars. Not so many years later, that same darkness would terrify me.

I recalled the vicious beatings handed out by Rafiq as I sobbed in my bedroom, hoping in vain that my dad would return from the dead and rescue me.

Later in life the darkness would protect me, hiding me under its cover as I fled the madrassa and the clutches of those who would have me fight for a very different army.

It was my turn for sentry. I strapped on the radio and the throat mic and climbed into the forward trench. I thought of Jessica, remembering when we first met and how beautiful she looked, even in the middle of a skydive. She was my heart and soul, my saviour and reason for living.

I didn't want to die out here, so far away from her. Being soldiers, we never talked about such personal matters but I knew deep down that many of the lads were thinking the same thoughts about their loved ones.

The minutes and hours ticked by. Behind me, some of the blokes were moving about, brewing up, chatting under their breaths. The overwhelming silence was making everyone jittery. I'd already relayed to the lads what I'd heard at the command post briefing given by the officer. We'd be crossing the border with the Yanks. Once into Iraq, our job would be to destroy every one of the Iraqi guns, tanks and mortar positions to our front. We'd have minutes to do this then we'd be gone, before our position could be discovered and blasted to hell.

"Let's get this shit over with," the officer said, "and get back home." My sentiments exactly.

23:00hrs. I'd stood down from sentry and was trying to get some kip in my usual billet by the ammo tent. Suddenly there seemed to be all sorts going on around me; blokes shouting and swearing, things being kicked over in a grab for clothing and equipment.

This was it – the scramble to arms.

Men and equipment, including the 105mm gun, had to be up and ready to go and within seconds we were moving forward in the Pinzgauer through a path cut in a 15ft high fence by British and American engineers, who had also bridged a deep ditch in order for us to cross the border.

We crept forward in the pitch-black, the tension almost unbearable. Would we be discovered by Iraqi troops and made to fight hand-to-hand in this alien landscape? Would we be cut to pieces by enemy artillerymen, our opposing numbers deep inside their own territory and holding all the aces? Might Iraqi jets swoop down on us in the dark, reducing us to dust?

Occasionally we saw flashes of fierce orange and red in the far distance. We assumed the main assault had begun, and that Allied air forces were already pounding their targets. Later we learned that Saddam had ordered the country's oil wells to be set ablaze so our forces couldn't secure them.

Finally, after what seemed like hours but was probably 30 minutes at the most, we were ordered to stop. Our regiment would be firing the first rounds of this war, not knowing where it would all lead and who we would be killing. For me, however, that last bit wasn't quite true. I knew who I'd be killing – fellow Muslims.

As we hauled the gun into position and unloaded the ammunition from the Pinzgauer I thought of those soldiers somewhere out in the darkness, soldiers of the same religion as me, who would be torn apart by our guns.

Ever since I could remember it had been drilled into me that to fight fellow Muslims was punishable by burning in hell.

The words of the religious police back home in Hawesmill rang in my ears: "If you join the British Army you will be an enemy of Islam. And you will be killed."

I paused for a moment. Would these guys really kill me if they got hold of me? Probably, but I wouldn't go down with a fight, and after seven years in the army I'd put up a good one. Equally, I might be killed by an Iraqi bullet or shell. If that happened, in the community's eyes justice would've been done.

I'd no more time to reflect. The sergeant was shouting at the top of his voice as he relayed orders coming from the radio: "Fire mission 6 guns. HE L106. PD charge three. Bearing 768 mils. Elevation 324mils. At my command. D30s in open. Five rounds fire of effect!"

Sweat poured down my face as I unloaded the high-explosive shell and watched it rammed up the barrel. The charge was then shoved in and the breech closed. We waited...waited...then...

"All guns – FIRE!"

I was straight into autopilot, hauling the shells over from the ammo tent and covering my ears as the guns roared into the night. The five shells were dispatched in seconds and we watched as they landed somewhere miles ahead, tearing into the enemy in a flash of flame and smoke. Again and again we fired, providing support to our guys on the ground and destroying enemy positions.

The Iraqis had been promised 'shock and awe' and were getting exactly that. Did I feel good about it? The answer is that I was a soldier doing my job.

This was what I'd trained for and I was under orders. Soldiers don't question what they're doing, especially in the heat of battle.

But when I saw the targets on fire, I had but one thought – that I'd helped to kill Muslims. It wasn't a thought I could dwell on for too long. Nonetheless, it was there.

As dawn came we pressed deeper into Iraq. In the early morning sunlight we saw weapons, uniforms and boots scattered everywhere, remnants of an army that appeared to have fled at the first shots. We all hoped this was a good sign, that Iraq would capitulate within weeks and we'd all be home and safe before too long. Further on we came across burned out tanks and bodies; the inevitable casualties of war, but no less shocking for that.

When ordered we would stop, fire off a few rounds, supporting the troops advancing in front of us then move on. The days and nights blended into one and none of us slept much, if at all. We travelled in convoy, heading north, and the effect of driving behind the shielded lights of the vehicle in front, in total darkness and for hours on end, was mesmerising. How we didn't crash I don't know. The effect was hypnotic, and it was extremely difficult not to let the mind wander in all sorts of weird directions. Keeping focus was difficult, especially on the road and once we'd stopped to rig up the gun.

We seemed to be in the middle of Iraq's rainy season and even now I can still picture the gun crews huddled in soaking, muddy trenches, waiting for our next set of orders. We could've been at the Somme or Ypres, yet in a way these were the least dangerous moments. Those came when the ground dried and the Iraqis were firing at us, trying to discover our positions. They'd drop a shell in our general direction, then look through binoculars to see where it had landed. If there was a secondary dust cloud generated by nearby movement they would recalibrate and bombard us.

This meant we had to stay completely still while under attack, which could be incredibly stressful.

We kept our heads down and tried not to think about what was coming towards us.

On one occasion I jumped into a slit-shellscrape as the 'Incoming!' alert was shouted, to find one of my colleagues huddled in a ball, crying, whimpering and praying. As the shells landed ever closer the ground shook and his distress became more and more intense. I whispered a few words of encouragement to him, but it was all I could do to hang on in there and try not to think of what might be about to happen to us all, i.e. that we'd be blown to pieces, our bodies buried under a mound of sand.

There were times when it was my turn to feel fear, bordering on panic. At one stage we came across a bullet-riddled car. Even from a distance we could see thick, congealing blood seeping from the door seals. We approached cautiously in case the vehicle was booby-trapped, and as we peered through the shattered windows we could see bodies inside, bodies of men, women and children, all dead. Perhaps they'd been caught in crossfire while fleeing, or deliberately targeted by one side or the other. I turned away and immediately vomited on the ground.

The combat part of the Iraq war lasted just over a month. Of course, the 'war' itself was far from over and what happened once Coalition operations ceased is well-documented.

In short, we might have won the war but the peace was badly mismanaged, leading to a complete destabilisation of this part of the Middle East and enabling the rise and rapid growth of militia groups, including the infamous Islamic State organisation.

So really, we didn't win anything all, but as the old piece of verse about soldiering goes, we weren't there 'to wonder why'. We just got on with the job which, for us, included a spell of peacekeeping operations.

For me, this was the most testing part of the whole operation. We toured towns and villages, trying to do the old 'hearts and minds' thing with the locals. Although there were differences, of course, the people we encountered looked similar, in dress and attitude, to those I'd encountered in Pakistan and Afghanistan. Their clothing had differences, but many men wore hats that closely resembled the kufi worn by Muslims across the world. Which in turn reminded me of my family at home in Hawesmill, and the fact that these Iraqi civilians and I shared the same religion.

I'd talk to kids who came up to us in the street, greeting them with the usual '*salaam alaikum*' and they'd be amazed to hear a British soldier pronouncing it the correct Arabic way. I didn't push the whole 'Muslim brother' thing; I'd escaped from that community and made a new family in the army. But this was where that escape had led me and as I got browner and browner under the desert sun, and a few of the lads made good-natured digs at me, I was once again aware of my differences in white Western eyes.

We were among the first troops to cross the border into Iraq, and among the first to return home to the UK following two weeks of downtime in Kuwait.

I was overjoyed to see Jessica; there had been many moments in Iraq when I wondered whether I'd make it home at all. She barely recognised me, as I was as brown as a nut and three stone lighter.

Fighting a war isn't always great for your health, but it's certainly an excellent way of losing weight.

Forbidden Soldier

With a month of leave to look forward to, Jessica picked me up from Aldershot and we drove to our new home on the south coast, me babbling all the way about what I'd seen and done during those intense few months.

I wandered about my new adopted home, watching people going about their daily lives. To them, it seemed that Iraq was just another slightly irritating headline on the news or in the paper. Sure, there had been lots of protests before the war started, but now? It was just another 'thing', something happening far away, out of sight and out of mind. People didn't really know what was going on over there, and cared even less. That was odd, but not really surprising.

Briefly, I returned north to see Jasmine, my sister, and also Helen, with whom I'd had a son, now aged 10. My sister wasn't in a particularly good place. She was now divorced and raising kids on her own, which wasn't easy in the community she lived in. Helen was OK. She'd been upset when I'd told her I was going to Iraq and was pleased to see me alive and well. It was a brief meeting. I hadn't really been part of their lives since we split up but she'd done an excellent job of raising our child.

Jasmine also knew I'd been to Iraq. We didn't talk about it much, knowing there would be questions if anyone had seen me arriving at her house. We did talk a lot about our mother. So many years had now gone by since she'd disappeared and we were still none the wiser about her whereabouts. One thing was certain, though; neither of us believed she was dead. We'd been told this by family over and over but it never rang true. Call it intuition or maybe just a small spark of hope; somehow, someday we both felt we would find her.

Back on the south coast, Jessica and I had a long talk.

We saw a firm future for ourselves, just getting on with our lives in contented happiness.

Like many army wives, Jessica was concerned that at some stage I'd have to return to the battlefield, either in Iraq or wherever else we were needed.

Having been on the front line once, I counted myself lucky that I'd survived the experience and I also felt I'd done my bit.

I'd gone into the army as a kid with a deeply troubled past, and the intervening seven years had sorted out a lot of the issues I was grappling with when I went in. I was far more confident in all areas and now had strength and resilience. Also, I'd met the woman I wanted to be with forever, and I didn't want anything to jeopardise that. With all that in mind, I made the decision to leave the army and, with many memories but no regrets, I gave in my notice and left, to retrain as a bodyguard. It was back to Civvy Street for me.

Pain will leave you when you let go.
Jeremy Aldana

Chapter Nine

Ghosts of the past

Forbidden Soldier

Once I'd qualified I joined a firm that worked right across the UK, particularly in the north of England, and often I found myself back in towns and cities only a matter of miles from Hawesmill. Despite everything I sort of missed the place; after all, it was where I'd partly grown up and, like pulling on an old coat, the familiarity was comforting.

After my work was finished for the day I'd make my way to whatever cheap B&B I was staying in for the duration of the job. But not before I drove around places like Blackburn, Preston, Hyde and Oldham, always keeping an eye out for something that might spark a forgotten memory from my past, perhaps offering up a clue that would put me on the trail of my long-lost mum.

As youngsters we spent time visiting various relatives or mosques across the north and, having driven around Oldham several times one evening, I spotted a house we'd travelled to many years before. I cannot recall whether this was the home of a relative, but part of this particular visit always included a donation of a fiver or a tenner which went into a funeral pot, so that when a relative died there would be money to pay for his or her service. Years had passed since I'd last been there but when I plucked up courage and knocked on the door I remembered the man who answered it.

I explained who I was, who my parents were and that I was trying to locate my mother.

"Hm," said the man, "yes, I remember them. Ahmed and Margaret. A good man. I was sad when he died. As for your mother…I don't know. That is the truth. They lived around here, you know…"

I pressed the man on where they lived and whether Mum might still be around. He seemed vague on the subject but not deliberately so – he either didn't know or couldn't remember. For a few days afterwards I cruised the streets of Oldham, looking for anyone who could be my mum. It was hopeless. So many middle-aged white women out there, and any one of them (or none) could've been her.

As I spent more and more time up north, it was inevitable that Hawesmill would draw me back at some stage. At first I was extremely reluctant to go anywhere near the place, remembering that the community elders had threatened me with death should I join the British Army. An instruction I'd obviously ignored wholeheartedly. Even so, I still had friends in the area – not least Jamie, Steve and their family – and, despite all odds, I made tentative contact with a couple of family members who weren't hostile towards me. These people (who I will not name) understood that I was different, and that what had happened to me when I was living in the town wasn't my fault. They were loyal to the family but unlike most of that lot, they understood the dynamics of the difficult situation Jasmine and I had found ourselves in.

Over the previous few years, and in the quieter moments when I wasn't busting a gut as a British soldier, I would think about what happened to us as kids, and particularly how I'd ended up in Pakistan.

Sometimes I'd question myself – *Did that really happen? Was I, an English kid, really sent to a madrassa?* – and often it felt as if all that history was part of someone else's life, not mine.

But it had happened to me, and a part of my psyche wanted to go back there, to walk once again in my own footsteps and see if I could lay the ghosts of the past to rest.

Anyway, to cut a long story short and after several conversations with my friendly relatives, I decided to accompany a couple of them on a three-week visit to the family in Pakistan. Looking back now, I do wonder whether I was in my right mind. I'd experienced hostility and imprisonment there, as well as witnessing an horrific murder. Plus, I'd been a member of the British Army and if I wasn't exactly flavour of the month when I went over there as a kid, now I would be a prime target for Islamic extremists who would enjoy nothing better than cutting off my head and sticking it on a spike somewhere prominent.

I think there's a part of me which has a real 'fuck it' element to it. When I was nothing more than a kid I climbed a wall to escape from a Taliban-run madrassa and legged it through a desert to safety. I became embroiled in drink and drugs then pulled myself out of it by volunteering to jump out of planes and fire large guns on the front line of a war. Then I met the love of my life and swapped adventure for close protection work and a happy domestic existence.

Deciding to go to Pakistan was another of these moments. Understandably, Jessica was not pleased. She was relieved that I'd survived the Iraq war and never considered that I'd put myself in danger again.

But at the time, I just didn't see it that way. I wanted to banish a few demons and the only way to do that, I thought, was to get up close to them.

So the tickets were booked and I was off to the village of Tajak via Islamabad, from where we would be picked up.

As soon as I got off the plane and settled in the back of the car that had arrived for us, I felt the memories come flooding back.

The people, the clothes, the buildings, the brightly-coloured trucks, the bustle and the busyness – very little had changed, except for a whole lot more satellite dishes around than in the past. The village itself looked smaller than I remembered, until I realised that I'd grown taller and was seeing things from a different perspective.

The house I was billeted in for the duration of the visit was very close to Aunty Alia's house, where I'd stayed the last time I'd been here. This was also the location of Ayesha's brutal gunning down by her husband Qaisar, my deeply religious cousin who I'd always liked and enjoyed playing cricket with. I had to steel myself to walk into that house again, given everything I'd witnessed that day, but I toughened up and stepped over the threshold, only because I wanted to see Alia.

She greeted me warmly, if a little warily. Obviously, she knew what I'd seen all those years ago, and how I'd been sworn to silence. We didn't talk about this incident or, indeed, my time at the madrassa which I think she felt guilty about. She had been assigned to protect me during my visit as a child, but had obviously allowed my reassignment to the madrassa to happen. But I was a man now, and in my heart I forgave her. She was under a lot of pressure at the time and as a woman in this society, she had to know her place.

I also visited my uncle Hussein, the kindly truck-driver I always thought looked like Father Christmas, complete with long white beard.

He was old now, suffering from dementia, and barely spoke a word. I was aware that years back I was supposed to be engaged to his young daughter and that, by rights, we'd be settled with a family of our own by now. However, the idea of having a child bride repelled me as much now as it did then, and I was glad I never gave in to family pressure.

I also went to see my father, or rather, his grave. Standing by the pile of stones scattered on the dusty earth, I was reminded of the last time I'd stood there, full of upset and anger. Upset at his sudden death and anger that we'd been abandoned to a family that didn't care what happened to us. Not long after, I'd been tricked into getting into a car before being taken to the madrassa by another uncaring relative. I prayed at my father's graveside, asking him and God to help me locate my mum and at least find out what had happened to her. But the quietness around this place, broken only by the eerie call of a large bird of prey floating many hundreds of feet above me, was symbolic of the silence that surrounded my mum's whereabouts. However hard I prayed, I felt I would never find her and I left the graveyard that day with the feeling that I'd come here for answers, only to discover more questions.

When I'd last been in Pakistan I'd understood a fair bit of the Pashto language spoken in this part of the country. Second time around, and not having mixed with native speakers for many years, I'd all but forgotten most of my second language.

But not everything. One day I was in a village shop with one of my cousins when the shopkeeper said something that made my ears prick up.

He was talking to my cousin while looking at me and when I heard the words 'British Army' mentioned I sensed an uncomfortable feeling creep into my stomach.

"What's he talking about?" I asked.

My cousin was evasive. "Erm, I'm not sure, bruv, to be honest, I think he's asking why you were in the army?"

The shopkeeper and my cousin continued talking, the discussion becoming quite heated.

By now I felt intensely uncomfortable, especially when I noticed other customers in the shop staring at me in silence. *Any of these guys could be Taliban*, I thought, knowing how word travels very quickly in small rural communities.

I motioned my cousin to leave the shop immediately, which we did, accompanied by increasingly hostile stares from the owner and customers. On the journey back to the house we were staying in I chewed over what had just happened and began to feel fear; real fear of the type I'd rarely experienced before, even in Iraq. Reality hit me square between the eyes and I realised I'd become encircled by danger. I felt a fool; I should've listened to Jessica and declined the invitation to come here. I was terrified that I would never see her again, and end up in a shallow grave by the side of some dirt road. This was a lawless area and even someone with connections, but also with links to the 'decadent' West and its armies, could quickly find themselves in deep trouble. Only a few short years later Osama Bin Laden was discovered hiding out in this area and killed by US Special Forces. My instinct about Taliban support here was spot on; if only I'd listened to it before I boarded the flight.

The minute I arrived at our compound I called the airline and rebooked my flight for the following day.

I needed to move quickly if I were to get out of Pakistan without plunging myself into further danger.

There were rumblings in the family and whispers in Pashto just out of earshot but even so, a cousin offered to drive me to Islamabad the next day and I've never been so pleased to board an aeroplane in my life. Maybe I was right about the level of danger I felt I was facing. Maybe I was wrong too, but I'm glad I didn't stay to find out.

I've never been back since, and I've no plans to do so. I discovered I didn't need to go there to find closure and put my past into perspective. All I really needed was to find my mother.

Back in England, my work was now almost exclusively based in the North West and it made sense for Jessica and me to move up there. We bought a three-bedroomed house on an estate in Wigan and settled down to a new life. Except we didn't really settle much. Jessica missed her family, who were all on the south coast, and despite my efforts the majority of my relatives in Hawesmill still didn't want much to do with me. Added to that was the ever-present threat of the community elders to kill me if they found out I'd joined the British Army. I figured that they must have had this confirmed by now, and I didn't want or need any hassle from these people. We weren't there long before we decided that our lives would be better spent down south, so we began the process of selling the place in Wigan and looking for jobs closer to where we wanted to be.

It was around this time that a friend of Jessica's heard my story during a visit to our house.

It wasn't a story I told to many people, but somehow the topic of Pakistan had come up in conversation and Jessica nudged me on to tell her friend a bit about what had happened to me since childhood. At the end of my account she sat open-mouthed.

"That is an incredible story," she said. "You should write a book. It'd get made into a film. You'd make millions!"

I used to joke that the only book I'd ever read was the Qur'an, but in reality it wasn't a joke. I could read and write perfectly well, but I just never did either unless it was necessary.

But her words planted an idea in my head. Could I really get all this down on paper? I figured that if I didn't try I'd never know, so I sat down with a laptop and started to write down everything I remembered from my past. I knew my words were a bit disjointed but I was amazed at how much I could remember once I got going. After a chapter or two I showed my efforts to Jessica's friend.

"It's good, Mo," she said, "really good. Keep at it. Maybe you should try to find a publisher."

Toward the end of 2009 we moved back down south and during this period I did as much research as I could about publishing, publishers, literary agents, editorial help and all the rest. And – to cut a long, involved and often frustrating story short – in 2011 I was given the opportunity by Harper Collins to tell my story, which I did in *Orphan of Islam*, published in the summer of 2012.

It has been translated into several languages and to date, has received almost 500 reviews online, the vast majority very favourable.

It hasn't yet been made into a film (I'm always hoping!) and I certainly haven't made millions from it, but

I'm very proud that my story made it to print, and with such a prestigious publisher. I could never have imagined that happening during my darkest days in the madrassa...

Happiness can exists only in acceptance
George Orwell

Chapter Ten

Life isn't a fairy-tale

Forbidden Soldier

Finally, I break the silence. 'What shall I call you – Margaret? Or Mum?'

'It's Mum,' she says, a huge smile on her face. 'It was always Mum. You'd better come in – we've got a lot to talk about.'

With these words, the final part of *Orphan of Islam* was concluded. But as I said in the introduction, many readers wanted to know what had happened to me after I returned from Pakistan as a teenager, and how I found my mother. Now that I've detailed the first part, here is what happened when I decided to make it my mission to track down my mother, even if it might have been to discover she was no longer around.

When I first began to write *Orphan of Islam* I quickly realised that we'd need some kind of conclusion, even if it might not be a happy one, or even one that had 'closure'. Over the years I'd made enquiries about and conducted searches for my mum, which had come to nothing. If I were to get any resolution to my story, it would have to come from this long and fruitless search.

On the recommendation of a friend I decided to enlist the help of a 'people-finder', a woman from Bristol called Joan Allen.

Joan, who has since died, was an expert in piecing together bits of information and scraps of memories to provide enough of a picture to start digging into records and archives.

I gave Joan everything I had or knew, and she assured me she'd do her best, while warning me it could take time, and that eventually I could be disappointed. That didn't matter to me; for more than 30 years there had been silence around the subject of my mum, so anything was better than nothing at all. And if there really was nothing at all, so be it. I was happy to wait.

After two days I received a call.

"I think you need to take a seat, Mo," Joan said. "I've found your mum."

I could hardly believe what I was hearing, and was so shocked that momentarily I couldn't speak.

"I know this will come as a shock to you," Joan said, "but once I got going it wasn't as difficult as I'd imagined."

"Is she alive?" I said, holding the receiver slightly away from my ear, almost not wanting to hear the bad news I expected.

"Yes, she is alive," Joan said calmly. "She's fine, I've spoken to her and she would like to speak to you."

Mum was alive. After all these years, and the countless hours I'd spent fretting, worrying and wondering, the woman who gave birth to us before disappearing from our lives was still around somewhere. I was utterly, completely gobsmacked.

"How did you find her?" I asked Joan.

"In the end, it wasn't that hard," she said. "You gave me her birth name, which you said was Margaret Firth."

"That's correct."

"Except that it isn't.

None of the Margaret Firths I looked up matched the other details you gave me. So I tried 'Margaret Frith' instead. And guess what? Within minutes I'd found her."

"So all these years she'd been missing, I could've found her if I'd known the correct name?"

"Probably. Sometimes it's as simple as that. Strangely enough, she's been living near Hyde all these years. She didn't go far."

My emotions started to get the better of me and I asked Joan to give me a few seconds. All this was hard to take in. For years I'd believed my mum was called one name. Now I'd discovered that it was slightly different, but that difference had been significant. Plus, I'd driven around Hyde, a town a few miles outside Manchester, a couple of times, thinking myself ridiculous for believing I'd see my mum walking past. And yet, that's exactly what could've happened, without my knowing. The truth was, she was hiding in plain sight less than 20 miles from Hawesmill. How weird.

Joan told me what happened when she broke the news to mum by phone. She introduced herself, told her to sit down and said that her son had been trying to trace her, and was she happy to carry on the conversation? Mum was, and Joan filled in some of the details I'd passed to her. Joan then said that if we were both happy, she'd arrange a conference call once I'd been given the news.

A day later the phone rang. It was Joan again, this time introducing me to a voice I couldn't recognise and had no memory of. A strong northern accent weathered by time and cigarettes.

"Hello, Moham. I can't really believe this is happening."

"Hello," I replied, not really knowing how to address this person.

She was my biological mother, yes, but 'Mum' sounded a bit familiar. Just at this moment.

"How are you, then? How's Jasmine?"

"We're fine, thanks," I replied. "It's good to hear your voice."

"Yours too. It's been a while."

The conversation was surreal in its normality. Jessica was at my side, urging me to ask Mum about this, that and that other. I couldn't, not yet. I needed time to process what was happening here; that I was talking to the woman who'd given birth to me and had disappeared from my life until now. I had so many questions, but now wasn't the time.

Joan seemed to sense this. Gently she interrupted our conversation and said that perhaps we could arrange to speak privately. We agreed, and the following day we talked again. This time it was longer, but still awkward. I struggled with not being able to put a face to the name. All I had to go on was the fact she was my mother. Anything else would have to be built from the ground up.

"Do you think we could meet?" I said hesitantly.

"Sure," she said. "I'd like that. Why don't you come up? Bring your wife. You can stay over. I've got room."

And so, a couple of weeks later I found myself standing outside a neat council house on an estate near Hyde. My heart was pounding, my palms were sweating and I felt like I was going to throw up. I was reminded of my first parachute jump – that feeling of hurling yourself into the unknown. I rang the bell, stepped back, and turned to look at Jessica who was standing beside me.

Through the glass I saw a white face framed by dark hair. The last memory I had of my mother was almost the same. The door opened. The face of a stranger greeted me, and yet...there was the warmest smile imaginable.

She cried as she said my name.

"It's you, Moham! It's really you! Oh my God..."

Quickly we were ushered inside. "I don't know what to call you," I said. And she replied with the words I'd wanted to hear for so many years, the words at the beginning of this chapter.

Mum's house was very neat and tidy. She was obviously a house-proud person. I noticed all the blinds in the front windows were down, which seemed odd, given it was daytime. She'd made a shepherd's pie and as she sat us down at her dining table we began to talk.

At first we were both nervous and hesitant. I wondered what was going through her mind. The son she'd last seen when he was just three years old was now a grown man, much taller than her. She knew nothing about me. I told her about my time in the army and she seemed pleased I'd served my country. Somehow that made her relax and she began to tell me something of the life we'd briefly had as a family.

As I suspected, she hadn't exactly been welcomed into Dad's family. There was hostility; not from everyone, but certainly from Dad's sister Fatima. This animosity forced Mum and Dad to move away. They had friends in Scotland, which is where they went and that was the reason I was born there.

They worked in various places, trying to create the kind of family they both claimed they wanted.

Dad, however, got a taste for whisky and started to become aggressive, which after a while turned into actual violence. They moved back to North West England and it was around that time she found out about his 'other' wife, the one in Pakistan with the children who would eventually move to Hawesmill and live with us following his death.

Not surprisingly, my parents split up soon after this revelation. Without her knowledge my father almost immediately took us to Pakistan and although she knocked on doors all over Hawesmill, as well as involving the police and a solicitor, there was a wall of silence surrounding our disappearance. Finally, she confronted Fatima, who told her we'd gone to Pakistan and had been killed in a car crash. It was a wicked lie and Mum knew it, but she couldn't prove otherwise and no-one was going to tell her the true story. She carried on searching but as days turned into months, and months became years, she got nowhere.

In the meantime she met a man who became her second husband and they had two kids. Again, there were problems of one sort or another, resulting in her husband's suicide. She never married again, instead throwing herself into work at a local factory where she was still employed. By the time we met she had grandkids and was evidently proud of them, showing us photo after photo. She asked if we had kids – perhaps she was hoping to meet other grandchildren, ones she never knew anything about.

We had to tell her that no, we didn't. The truth was that we so desperately wanted children, but it just wasn't happening. And time was ticking for us.

"It's not been an easy life," she said, "but I've got through it.

I never stopped thinking about you, you know," she said. "I never believed you were dead. I thought you'd gone to Pakistan for ever. I never thought I'd see you again. Anyway, tell me about your life…"

I told her everything – the cruelty, the beatings, the second trip to Pakistan, the kidnapping to a madrassa, the escape. She could barely believe what she was hearing. At certain points in the telling I became very emotional. We certainly drank a lot of strong tea that day. She hugged me, telling me everything would be alright. I wasn't sure what she meant; there had been a lot that wasn't alright, not in the slightest. Was she hinting at a secure future for us both, one in which my sister and I would have an unusual but solid relationship with the mother we never knew?

Before I went to bed, I asked her why the blinds had been drawn when I arrived. Just asking this question made her glance furtively from side to side. She explained that it was a very white neighbourhood with a lot of residents who didn't take kindly to people like me. In other words, Pakis.

"If they see I've got an Asian bloke in here, they'll want to know what's going on," she said.

"Oh, right."

"Yeah, and while I'm on the subject, I'll take you out for lunch tomorrow but you'll have to park your car round the corner and wait in it for me to come out. People talk…"

I guessed that Mum had been talked about enough over the years and didn't want any more gossip. She'd told her kids many years ago that she'd had another family, but apart from that she'd never let on to anyone about us and it seemed she wanted to keep it that way.

The following day we went to a pub, as planned, and as usual I chatted away about anything and everything. Mum, however, was quieter. Perhaps she was only just absorbing the impact of our discovery, and of everything that had happened to us. Possibly, though, she'd heard just about everything she wanted to hear. Before we left for the long journey south she thrust a carrier bag into my hand.

"What's this?" I said.

"Easter eggs," she replied. "That's what you give your kids when Easter comes. Don't eat them before you get home!"

"I won't, Mum," I said, pleased to obey the first instruction I'd had from her in a very long time.

Then we hugged. "Well, keep in touch," she said.

"Of course I will!" I said, surprised by her words. Was that what mums always said to their kids as a form of goodbye? I was expecting something more personal, especially after all this time. But 'keeping in touch' it was and for now, that would have to do.

Mum had also asked me how much it had cost to employ Joan to reunite us. I told her that the cost didn't matter, and not to worry about it. When we reached home I rang her to say we'd arrived safely, and that it was lovely to have met her.

"Have you eaten the chocolate eggs yet?" she said.

"No," I replied. "You told me not to."

"Open the big one now, and look down the side of the box."

I did as I was instructed and pulled out an envelope. Inside it was cash. £250.

"You shouldn't have done," I said.

"I know I shouldn't," she replied, "but I have done anyway. Enjoy it."

For weeks afterwards we messaged daily, ringing each other a couple of times a week. Nothing heavy or serious, just trying to catch up on all the years we'd missed.

We talked about possibly going on holiday and generally spending more time together.

She still didn't feel quite like 'my mum', or how I'd expected a mother to be, though I knew we had a long way to go and that I could hardly expect to have what might pass for a 'normal' mother-son relationship, given we were more or less strangers.

After a month or two Mum's replies to my messages became shorter, terser.

"Hi! How are you doing?"

"I'm good, thanks."

"Hi, Mum, hope everything's OK with you?"

"Yep."

And so on, until one day I received a reply to a friendly enquiry.

"Mo, you don't need to text me all the time. I'm OK, you're OK. Just enjoy your life."

I backed down quickly, realising that perhaps I'd come on too strong, too quickly. But from that point onwards our conversations – by text or phone – became fewer. The painful truth was that Mum was backing away from me. That she'd been 'found' was enough for her, as well as the fact that I was OK. She saw that I'd made a life for myself away from the family that had persecuted us both. I was safe and well, and she was happy with that.

I can't pretend that I wasn't hurt. All the years wondering about her, where she might be, why she'd left us, the effects of that abandonment…and now this, a mother who didn't really want to be a mum to me.

Perhaps I was naïvely hoping that we'd spend time catching up on those lost years while making new memories; good memories that in time would erase the bad ones.

Having assumed that any family that wasn't like mine was automatically a happy one, I was shocked to discover that blood isn't thicker than water after all. Margaret Frith was someone I had something in common with, but that's all this particular bond amounted to.

She'd loved us then lost us, and had to find a way to go on. When we turned up again, she was either unable or unwilling to change the strategies she'd used to cope with that loss.

I felt sad for us all. It should've been a happy ending, and it should have been the payoff that the readers of *Orphan of Islam* were hoping for and demanding. Sadly, it wasn't and isn't.

I'm sorry to disappoint you, but life isn't a fairy-tale. Happy endings don't happen regularly, except in feel-good fiction. The course of true life doesn't always run smoothly. I hold out for a good relationship with my mum but after almost ten years since we first met, and never having met again, I realise that I'm being somewhat optimistic. I would also like my sister to find some peace and happiness in her life. She has been through a lot – but that is her story, and only she can tell it. In brief, I can say that she's now remarried and is in a happier situation as a result.

She is a successful businesswoman living in Yorkshire and yes, she did meet Mum, though I was not with her when this meeting took place, and what went on between Jasmine and Mum is their business.

Jasmine still retains strong connections with the family in Hawesmill, whereas I have very little to do with them.

I'm still the black sheep; or, perhaps more accurately, the black-and-white sheep. I'm sure they thought they were doing the right thing by us as kids.

The events I wrote about in *Orphan of Islam* happened a long time ago and things have changed. But, in the case of tight-knit communities such as the one I grew up in, perhaps not for the better. The religious fundamentalism which was creeping in when I lived there has tightened its grip.

People are even more cautious and afraid of the outside world. The events of 9/11 did no-one any favours, least of all the impoverished, defensive and misunderstood Asian communities of the north of England.

I had it pretty bad, but I'll bet a king's ransom others have had it far, far worse since.

Had I stayed I'd have probably knuckled down, got married, had kids, become religious and grown a beard, and might have a job as a waiter or a taxi driver, if I'd been lucky. I might never have been fully accepted but perhaps in time the community would've budged up and let me in. It would've been a small life, for sure, and one in which everyone knows their place. Perhaps, in time, that would've suited me. Though I doubt it.

I'm proud of what I've achieved. I've done things I never could've imagined doing. I've jumped in with two feet and largely, it's paid off. Writing *Orphan of Islam* changed my life in ways I couldn't have anticipated.

People all over the world have read it, and have contacted me to say how much it helped them with their own struggles, whatever they may be.

Thinking that my story has helped someone makes me feel good.

That was my reason for writing the book and it's been successful from that perspective.

About that happy ending…maybe I was wrong. Things don't always end the way we want them to. So maybe it's better to hope for an alternative ending, one that might not quite hit the mark in accordance with the fairy-tale, but is, at least, something of a conclusion.

As I've mentioned, soon after I left the army Jessica and I talked about having children, but it just wasn't happening. We even tried IVF, with no success. This was hugely disappointing for us both. However, we planned to adopt a child in the future and in the meantime just carry on with life.

About five years ago we went on a fortnight's holiday to Antigua, which would've been great had Jessica not felt unwell the whole time.

When we arrived home she saw her GP, who suggested she take a pregnancy test. She laughed and almost didn't bother. But she did. It came back positive.

It was a shock to start off with but very quickly I realised I had a chance to bring up a child and love him, having missed pretty much all of my older son's upbringing. Somehow I'd been gifted the opportunity to put that right and bring up a child in a loving, caring environment. Throughout the pregnancy, the scans and the birth, I always considered what my parents must have gone through and how difficult it must have been for them. Jessica gave birth to a boy, and we couldn't have been prouder parents.

Like all couples, we've had our ups and downs. Being new parents is tough, especially when you're that bit older and the sleepless nights and constant demands are harder to deal with.

As happens, things began to get on top of us and there was talk of us splitting up, with me moving out. I had an awful lot of thinking to do during this time, and I did not want history to repeat itself. Jessica and I worked hard to repair our relationship and now we're stronger as a couple, and a family, than we ever were.

Now, our son is about the same age as I was when we were removed to Pakistan that first time.

It kills me to think of him disappearing from our lives and the impact that would have on us.

For that, I forgive my mother for not being the person I hoped she would be. She did her best, under extreme circumstances, which is all any of us can do. Now we have our own miracle, we are determined that he will grow up in a happy, stable environment in which he will be free to be who he wants, without interference or castigation. He is the child of an orphan; an orphan who will never forget how it feels to be this way.

Forbidden Soldier

The Recruit

Forbidden Soldier

Chapter One

Forbidden Soldier

The sun was setting over Lashkar Gah, Afghanistan, as Corporal Darren Reeves stepped out from the bustling mess tent, slid a single cigarette from his shirt pocket, and made his way towards one of the watchtowers that dotted the camp's high perimeter wall. He turned the thin paper cylinder over and over in his fingers as he walked trying to imagine Andrea's disapproving expression if she could see him holding it.

Five months into the tour, Darren had begun to have trouble clearly picturing his wife's face. At first he found the whole thing ridiculous. Of course he knew what his own wife looked like and he had plenty of photos, but he had lost the ability to summon her image to his mind. Perhaps it was just a by-product of the stress and sleep deprivation that every soldier in the camp suffered in one way or another. This strange amnesia was his way. This was his punishment.

The boys had been no help of course: feigning concern that he might be going blind and forcing him to try on Hicksey's thick, 'jam jar bottom' glasses amidst gales of laughter. They'd also suggested that his wife was actually really ugly, that he was trying to make himself believe otherwise because he didn't want to go home to her. The banter made him feel better, but it didn't make him any more able to picture Andrea. The only thing that helped was imagining her expressions in certain situations.

Her guilty smile when she walked through the door after buying something she shouldn't have. The mingled surprise and exasperation when she'd topple over while pulling on her socks, which happened most mornings. And most of all, her disapproving frown whenever Darren put a cigarette in his mouth.

He had promised her that he would quit before he came home, and true to his word he hadn't smoked a cigarette in months. But when he realised that he could see Andrea's face clearly anytime he wanted by simply screwing a smoke between his lips and closing his eyes, he had borrowed this one from Marine Baines and carried it around with him everywhere.

The watchtower creaked as Darren took its narrow metal steps two at a time. The American guard at the top jerked his head upwards in welcome, but before either of them could say anything a single wailing voice floated through the air from the town beyond. Then another. And another. The evening call to prayer rang out from half a dozen tall, thin minarets into the red evening sky, the voices joining and mingling to create an eerie cacophony of sound. To a person of the right faith, the scene might have been beautiful. Darren found it creepy as hell.

'I wish they wouldn't do that,' muttered Baines, shifting the wad of tobacco in his mouth and spitting into the sand down below.

'No kidding,' Darren replied.

'You boys headed home tomorrow, huh?' asked the American, looking Darren up and down.

'Yeah.'

'Lucky bastard.'

'I guess.'

'You guess?!' The Yank stared at him in disbelief. 'I'd give my left nut to be on my way home tomorrow. The right one too, matter-of-fact, long as my dick still works I don't give a shit anymore.'

'That's the spirit,' said Darren, thumping Baines on the shoulder before turning to head back down the watchtower steps. He knew he should be more excited about going home, but the truth was he hadn't let himself think about it enough for the realisation to set in. A few months ago, home was all Darren could think about. He'd had two weeks' leave coming up, and had been looking forward to it more than he'd looked forward to anything in his life. But then the leave was cancelled. No replacements available, they said; stretched too thin. For the last few weeks Darren had refused to let himself think about going home in case it got cancelled again. He would only believe it when he finally saw his loved ones with his own two eyes.

Darren had made it maybe twenty feet from the wall when he heard the Yank call out again.

'Well I hope your wife is a dog!'

Baines has a big fucking mouth, he thought, but didn't reply.

As he trudged back towards the barracks, Darren noticed two of the heavily-armoured Jackals roll out from their compound and head for the camp's main gate. Something was going down, but he couldn't bring himself to care what it might be. It was someone else's problem now.

'Daz! Come on!' Geordie Private Ed Morris smacked Darren on the arm as he ran past.

'Not now, Ed,' said Darren. 'I just want to sleep.'

'They've blown up a plane!' Ed called over his shoulder before disappearing into the rec room: a large, semi-permanent tent.

'They'... what?' Darren scanned the skies. If anything exploded within a hundred miles of the base, they'd hear it. What on earth was Ed talking about? Then he noticed more people running towards the rec room and his heart fell. This wasn't going to be good news.

The rec room, a crowded place at the best of times, was packed full of soldiers like sardines in a tin, all craning their necks to see the television on the far wall. It was showing footage of a thick column of black smoke rising some distance away from the camera, and at first Darren couldn't figure out what he was seeing. Maybe he did need glasses after all. He pushed his way closer, squinting at the screen, and as the landscape came into focus his stomach turned over. There was no mistaking the green fields and rows of trees under that grim grey sky. That wasn't Afghanistan. It was England.

'What happened?' he asked the man next to him, a vaguely familiar face from another regiment.

'Dunno mate, I just got here myself. They said--'

'Shut up!' yelled a voice behind them. 'Where's the fucking remote? Turn it up.'

There was a scramble down in front of the television, then the volume began to rise, and the room fell silent.

'Eye witness reports,' said a plummy female voice over the live video, 'are telling us that a VC10 Tristar aircraft carrying as many as a hundred and twenty British soldiers has exploded shortly before take-off at RAF Brize Norton. We have no further details at this time, but we're going to stay live--'

'So much for our replacements,' said a voice to Darren's left.

'Fuck!' yelled one to the right. Within seconds the crowded room was buzzing like a nest of angry wasps.

'Of course it's terrorists!' said a Cockney private from Darren's regiment by the name of Garland. 'Planes don't just blow up on their own, do they?'

'You know a lot about aeronautical engineering, do you, Garland?' snapped a sergeant with a flat, leathery face. A few people laughed.

'I know they don't just blow the fuck up!'

'That's enough now,' barked the sergeant, trying to take charge of the anxious crowd, 'don't some of you have duties to attend to?'

'I'm telling you,' Garland went on, 'this is what they do - the fucking ragheads. They wait till you're all packed into a nice tight space and then they fucking blow you up.'

'I said that's enough!'

Darren stared at the television for a moment longer, then looked around at the faces of the others watching. Their reactions, he saw, were the same as his. Shock, numbness, helplessness, despair at the thought that not only were soldiers dead, but that their loss might mean another round of cancelled leave for everyone.

Two more people ducked into the already crowded tent and began pushing their way into the middle of the room for a better view.

At first Darren paid them no mind, but when one of the men stopped just a few feet from him he noticed the dark skin and tell-take facial hair of a local.

One of the interpreters? Darren's mind had been pre-occupied by the events on the television, but it was working again now, rushing to process what was wrong with the scene. The dark-skinned man was wearing a British Army uniform. Interpreters usually had only a mish-mash of leftover gear and almost always American as they had more to spare.

The man watched the television for a few seconds, then he seemed to feel Darren's stare on him and turned to face him. As their eyes met, a chill ran down Darren's spine. He saw hatred that burned so powerfully it seemed to cause the surrounding air to shimmer. The man reached up and pulled open his jacket.

When he caught site of the tangle of wires beneath it, Darren realised what was happening and knew at once that there was nothing he could do. He turned away, brought the raggedy cigarette to his lips, closed his eyes, and silently said goodbye to his wife.

Chapter Two

Forbidden Soldier

'They're definitely in there.'

'How many?'

'Could be as many as a dozen.'

'Fuck me.'

'You're already getting fucked mate, that's why you're here.' Geoff Robbins slapped Ethan Blake on the shoulder before swinging round to position himself behind the General-Purpose Machine Gun (GMPG) at the front of the Jackal. They were sitting at a crossroads in the town of Kariz, just a few miles from Lashkar Gah. The sun had set now and, though there were buildings all around them, not a soul could be seen. This was not a good sign. Many of the locals weren't fans of the NATO forces here, but they didn't usually hide from them unless something was up.

'I hate surprises,' muttered Ethan, peering through the sights of his weapon.

'Really?' asked Dave Wells from the driver's seat. 'What about a surprise birthday party?'

'You think they've got a fucking cake in there?' said Geoff, nodding at the windowless building in front of them. The morning's intelligence briefing had identified it as a possible shelter for suicide bombers arriving from across the Pakistan border, and some asshole junior officer had decided to send his lads to investigate.

'Think we should find out,' replied Ethan, reaching for his Minime light machine gun.

'Stay where you are, you muppet,' snapped Geoff. But Ethan had already grabbed his weapon and climbed down from the vehicle.

'Ethan, mate, what the fuck are you doing?' said Dave. 'We're just supposed to scout the place.'

'That's what I'm doing,' said Ethan calmly. 'You don't have to come.'

'We won't,' said Geoff. Ethan shrugged, flicked the safety catch off his weapon, and began to walk slowly, yet purposefully, towards the building.

A breeze swept through the crossroads with a low, haunting whistle, whipping a thin haze of sand up all around him. It felt like the desert itself was trying to warn Ethan that this was a bad idea. He gripped his weapon tighter and tried to ignore it. 'It's all in your mind,' he told himself. 'You've just been out here too long...'

He was maybe ten yards from the door when it creaked open. Ethan froze, feeling the trigger of his Minimi, and tasting the adrenaline in the back of his mouth. The air was still for seconds that felt like minutes and then, with a strangled cry, figures burst from the open door and sprinted straight for him.

'FUCK!' Ethan fired off an instinctive burst from his weapon before breaking and sprinting back towards the Jackals. He had no idea if he'd hit anything. He had seen at least four or five faces before he turned to run, all twisted up in screams of hatred. And all of them wearing bomb vests.

Geoff was shouting something, but with the blood pounding in his ears and the screams close behind him, Ethan couldn't immediately make it out.

'... Down! Get down, you prick! DOWN!'

Ethan saw Geoff and Dave, then the three guys on the second Jackal, all pointing their machine guns straight at him, and he understood. With a desperate effort, he threw himself forwards and rolled towards them, hearing the General Purpose Machine Guns (GPMGs) and fifty-cal erupt even before he hit the ground. But there was something else too. A roaring sound. Ethan lay still and closed his eyes, waiting for one of the bombs to go off.

He couldn't help remembering what an IED could do. He had seen for himself the deadly aftermath of an explosion; men's bodies reduced to shredded lumps of char-grilled meat, smoking in the hot sun, scorched blood broiling in the desert sand. He wondered if he would feel any pain before he died.

But the blast never came. And now there was yet another sound above him. Was it... helicopter blades? Ethan opened his eyes and raised his head. The first thing he saw was the face of one of the suicide bombers barely ten feet from him. He was just a boy, no more than fourteen or fifteen years old, his eyes open in shock. Then as Ethan pulled himself to his feet, he saw what had stopped the boy in his tracks. His body had been torn in two, the lower half shredded and sprayed right across the junction. A GPMG didn't do that.

Ethan looked up, and saw a black Chinook helicopter hovering above them, spraying the compound with its 7.62 mm six-barrelled machine gun. He glanced towards Geoff and Dave for an explanation, but they looked as dumbfounded as he was. The compound exploded in a huge fireball, sending chunks of stone high into the air.

'I want one,' said Geoff simply as Ethan climbed back up into the vehicle.

'Who the fuck are these guys?' asked Dave. Ethan shrugged. The whole patrol watched in disbelief as the Chinook turned in the air and then came down gracefully in the middle of the crossroads. A second Chinook hovered above, armed and ready to take out any threat. Then a man wearing a plain grey suit stepped out of the Chinook, straightened his tie, and approached the Jackals.

'He looks like a bank manager,' said Geoff. 'You behind on your mortgage payments again, Ethan?'

'Well, you know, if they paid us a proper wage-'

'Are you Ethan Blake?' asked the man in the suit. He was well-spoken, with the hint of a Yorkshire accent.

'Who's asking?'

'I don't have time for games, lad,' said the suited man. 'I need you to come with me right now.'

'Now hold on,' interrupted Geoff, 'I don't know who the hell you are, but we have orders. We're to report back to our Lieutenant at--'

'Your Lieutenant is dead,' said the man. 'You're right though, both Jackals need to return back to base immediately. But I need him,' he jerked a thumb at Ethan, 'or more people are going to die.'

'You what?' said Geoff. 'Lieutenant. Larson...'

'I just gave you fresh orders, sergeant,' snapped the man. 'Corporal Blake, follow me please.'

Ethan looked at Geoff, who shrugged.

'You'd better go mate,' said Dave. 'He might repossess your house.'

'See you later, I guess,' said Ethan, climbing down from the Jackal.

'Home in two weeks, right?' said Geoff.

'If I've still got one,' replied Ethan. He picked up his weapon and followed the mysterious suited man to the rear of the Chinook.

Forbidden Soldier

Act of Vengeance

Forbidden Soldier

Chapter One

Forbidden Soldier

August, 2008

Tazagram, Northern Pakistan

Omar Ramay was glad he had listened to his parents. If he'd paid attention to the news, his friends – and some of his teachers – he would have stayed in Bradford. All they saw was the negative: that Pakistan, the north in particular, was a dangerous place afflicted by war, terrorism and criminality. Thankfully, Omar's parents knew different. Of course, there were dangers, but in most parts of the country ordinary people lived out ordinary lives. And Tazagram was very ordinary. In fact, Omar might even have considered it boring – had he not met Wasim.

Wasim came from a family who lived on the edge of Tazagram. They were poor folk with only a fraction of the land owned by Omar's relatives. As far as he could tell, the only livestock they possessed were a few scrawny goats. Omar still wasn't sure what had happened to Wasim's father but from his anguished reaction when the subject came up, he'd decided not to ask again. Wasim had an older brother and they both worked as labourers for neighbouring farmers. Omar had been out for an evening walk with his parents when he'd first seen them: heading home, covered in dust, with shovels over their shoulders.

The next time he saw Wasim, Omar was alone. He was a week into his holiday and still unused to the blistering summer heat. With his mother helping his aunt in the kitchen and his father discussing politics with the menfolk, Omar took himself off to a nearby river to cool down. As he swam idly around, he heard a splash. Wasim had dived in off a rock and was as surprised as Omar when he surfaced. The two exchanged greetings and continued their conversation in Pashto. Omar only ever spoke the language at home when in England but had used little else while in Tazagram; he was making good progress.

The young men discovered that they were both fifteen and from then on met up regularly. Wasim came for dinner at the compound owned by Omar's family and in return showed him how to fish. Omar gave Wasim a couple of books he had bought in Karachi and Wasim took him up a nearby hill which offered spectacular views of the area. Omar had plenty of spare money and – though he didn't tell his parents – would often buy sweets and bottles of Coke for his friend. When not walking or swimming, they would borrow two rickety bikes from Omar's uncle and race through the narrow alleys of the village.

Omar had only a week of his holiday left when he and Wasim decided to make an expedition to a prime fishing spot. It was a two-hour round trip and Omar's parents only agreed because they knew he would be safe with his streetwise new friend. Wasim worked in the morning but had the afternoon free. Fortunately, there was a bit of cloud to protect them from the worst of the sun.

Omar and Wasim were the same height and therefore walked at a similar pace.

Wasim was lean and strong from his daily regimen of work while Omar stayed fit from football and swimming back in Bradford.

Both wore the traditional salwar kameez but their footwear was very different. For Omar, Nike Air trainers; for Wasim, a pair of threadbare sandals that didn't slow him down at all. They took it in turns to carry Omar's backpack, which contained water bottles, fishing net, knife, lighter, frying pan, rice and some tin bowls. They planned to cook and eat whatever they caught and walk back in the cool evening.

The first part of the journey took them along a minor road. They were about to turn off onto a track when they heard the rumble of a vehicle behind them. They had seen only a few since leaving the village so both turned around. Leaving a trail of dust behind it and approaching at some speed was an old-looking van. The vehicle slowed as it got closer and Omar didn't like the suspicious look upon Wasim's face. The van passed them, then pulled in just ahead. Omar noticed that all the windows were blacked out.

'Wasim?'

'It's okay.'

But Omar could hear the tension in his friend's voice. He looked around – there wasn't a building or person in sight and they were at least three miles from Tazagram.

The front doors of the van flew open and two men jumped out. They were both bearded and wore dark robes. Omar wasn't sure what scared him most; the looks in their faces or the rope the man to the left was holding.

'Run!' yelled Wasim.

But by then the man to the right had pulled out a revolver. He aimed at it at the boys and grinned.

'Come,' said the man with the rope. The two strangers were calm and relaxed, as if this was nothing new to them.

Omar couldn't see that he had any choice. He started walking but stopped when he realised Wasim hadn't moved.

The man with the gun took several steps forward and aimed the barrel of the gun at Wasim's knee. 'Now.'

Wasim and Omar complied. The man with the rope turned Wasim around and began tying his hands. Omar was tall for his age but the gunman was at least six inches taller. He stank of sweat and his pale eyes seemed utterly devoid of humanity. Omar had never felt such fear; his throat was so tight he didn't think he could talk.

The gunman opened the rear of the van. The other man took Omar's pack (which contained his phone) and began tying his hands.

'Keep quiet.' The gunman shoved Wasim towards the van. Inside was a third man who hauled Wasim up and pushed him onto the floor. Omar winced as the rope cut into his wrists. Then he too was bundled inside and shoved down beside Wasim. The door slammed shut. The third man slumped down opposite them and casually inspected the new arrivals.

Omar looked forwards. The other two men climbed in, joining a fourth behind the wheel. As the van drove away, Omar noticed the last occupant, a boy of about twelve cowering between Wasim and the front seat. His hands were tied and his mouth was covered with tape. His unblinking eyes projected nothing but terror.

Two hours later, Omar found himself with the other boys in a cramped, grimy outhouse. He guessed the van must have driven at least fifty miles and he had glimpsed little but sky and mountains through the windows. Wasim had tried to speak once but a punch from the man watching them had put an end to that. Omar watched as Wasim now wiped his still-bleeding mouth with his sleeve.

'Say something!'

Wasim had tried to engage with the third boy but even though the gag had been removed, he would not say a word. The trio had been told to be quiet but it sounded like their captors had moved away after locking them in. As they were bundled out of the van, Omar had noted they were at a remote farmhouse: nothing more than a collection of ramshackle clay buildings built around a well.

'Who do you think they are?' he asked.

'How should I know?' said Wasim. 'Here, try and undo it.'

He got onto his knees and turned so that his tied hands were facing Omar.

Omar turned to help.

'Could be kidnappers,' added Wasim.

That didn't make much sense to Omar. If they had just taken him, perhaps – he had a comparatively rich family – but Wasim's relatives had nothing and the other boy looked poor too.

Omar reached out and touched Wasim's fingers. After a bit of trial and error, he found he could reach the ropes. He began trying to untie them.

'Stop.'

It was the first and only word out of the boy's mouth. Omar turned and saw him shaking his head emphatically.

Wasim muttered a curse. 'You do nothing if you want, fool. At least we're trying.'

After about five minutes, Omar had to stop – his fingers were sore from the effort.

'Keep going,' insisted Wasim. 'They could come back any time.'

Omar did so; and soon began to make progress. His aching fingers pulled one knot loose, then the second, then the third. At last, Wasim was free. Now it was Omar's turn and Wasim soon had the ropes off.

'You'll have to give me a lift. I'll try for the window.'

There was only one: high, small and protected by a wire mesh.

'We'll never get through that,' said Omar.

'I've got through smaller gaps in my time. Come on!'

Omar hurried over and stood below the window while Wasim kicked off his sandals. Omar gave him a leg up and in seconds he had both feet on his friend's shoulders.

'Well?'

'I can get this mesh off, no problem. The wall is weak too, we might even knock some of the clay out. I think we can do–'

Suddenly the weight was off Omar's shoulders and Wasim landed next to him. 'They're coming. Quick.'

Wasim and Omar wrapped the rope round their wrists as best they could. They turned away from each other once more and Omar managed to tie two knots on Wasim's bindings before they heard the men approach. They sat down against the wall as the bolt was pulled back.

The door swung open. Omar pressed his hands together and prayed the captors wouldn't notice he was free. Two of the men walked in: the one who had sat with them and the driver, who was holding a large knife with an engraved wooden handle. Omar hadn't seen many drunk men in Pakistan but he had seen plenty in Bradford and he knew the signs. The driver aimed the knife at the young boy. The second man pulled him up off the ground and dragged him back through the door. With a sick grin for the remaining captives, the driver shut the door and bolted it shut behind him.

As soon as the voices and footsteps faded, Omar was back on his feet. 'Come on. Quickly!'

'What about him?' said Wasim.

'We can't wait – this might be our only chance!'

'We can't leave him here alone. He's even younger than–'

They could hear him from inside the farmhouse, crying, begging and pleading. The men were laughing.

'No! Please, no!'

Omar and Wasim listened. One of the men began grunting like a pig. Only now did Omar fully realise what was happening.

Footsteps outside. Omar lowered himself to the floor beside Wasim. The bolt was opened, then the door. The gunman entered, pistol in hand. He looked as drunk as the others as he lurched across the room then stopped above the boys, swaying. His slow-moving gaze switched between them.

Omar looked at the floor. *Not me. Not me. Please, not me.*

'You – get up.'

He couldn't even look. Then the gunman reached down and hauled Wasim up by his arm. Wasim tried to resist but the captor pointed his gun between his eyes and hissed curses at him. He dragged Wasim towards the door and outside. The last thing Omar saw of his friend were his eyes. The message was clear: *wait for me.*

But Omar waited only a minute before he stood and shook the rope off. He could hear more noise from the house, even some music playing now.

He reckoned the window was about eight feet off the ground. There was nothing in the room he could use to climb on; no way of getting up without help.

Then he spied the pile of dust in the corner where the boy had been sitting. And the faded plastic bag and the used matches.

And the rusty nails. There were three of them, each about ten centimetres long with a large, square head.

Omar grabbed them and began scraping away the clay below the window, about four feet off the ground. He had soon made a hole wide enough for all three nails. He pushed them in as far as he could, then took off one of his trainers. Using it as a hammer, he knocked the nails in, leaving about a third poking out for a foothold. Much of the surrounding clay had come loose. He could only hope it would hold.

Omar put his trainer back on. He took a running jump and reached with both hands for the edge of the window. One hand got a grip but he lost it as his foot searched for the nails. He dropped to the floor. Shutting out Wasim's cries, he tried again.

This time he got both hands on the edge and his scrabbling foot found the nails.

With his foot half-supporting him, he could now use one hand to pull at the mesh. He shook it until the frame began to come free of the crumbling clay. Gritting his teeth, Omar kept at it until the whole thing came out. He discarded it over his shoulder.

By stretching high, he could now get his elbows almost onto the near edge of the window and his fingers over the far edge. The energy of desperation coursed through him as he levered himself upward until his elbows were resting on the window.

He wriggled up and forward and somehow got his shoulders through. He was now lying across the window, upper body outside, legs inside. The farmhouse was over to his right, about twenty feet away. Thankfully, the music was now louder and covering the other sounds. The dusty ground below looked a long way down and he could only get out headfirst. He knew he might injure himself but there was no other way and no time to spare.

Omar wriggled forward again until his knees were over the window and his weight pulled him down. He made himself twist as he fell and at least spread the impact as he thumped onto the ground. The force of the landing winded him. He lay there on his back helplessly for a while, sucking in breaths until he was able to stand. His shoulder was burning with pain but he knew he could move.

He struggled to his feet and set off. With a last look at the farmhouse, he rounded the corner of a fenced yard and looked out at a distant road.

There was a sign no more than half a mile away; at least he would know which way to go.

I'll be back with help, Wasim, I promise.

Forbidden Soldier

Once he reached the track that led to the road, Omar ran like he had never run before.

Chapter Two

Forbidden Soldier

March, 2016

Merville Barracks, Colchester, England

The NAAFI bar was quiet. Omar knew most of his Company were away on exercise in Jordan, so he decided to visit Colchester, where a few familiar faces were still kicking around. He'd been given two weeks' leave and had no idea what his next posting would be. His valuable combination of skills had seen him undertake various duties during the last two years of his career with B Company, Special Forces Support Group. As a fluent Pashto speaker, most of his assignments had involved supporting 22 SAS Regiment and, on two occasion, M15. He had been deployed in Afghanistan, Iraq, Syria and Yemen.

Sitting on a stool by the bar, Omar took a sip of the lager he had just ordered. He had been back with his family in recent days and therefore unable to drink alcohol. He still considered himself a Muslim but beer had been a part of his life ever since he'd joined up. The taste – and the surroundings – were familiar and reassuring. And he felt even better when Johnno walked in, right on time as usual.

Omar stood and shook his hand. He and Sergeant Matthew Johnson had endured training together and stood proudly beside each other when they'd finally received their maroon berets and coveted "wings". Though they'd never actually served in the same unit, they met up whenever they could and kept in touch via email. Johnno was a short, wiry man with a winning smile.

'Sarge.'

'Sarge,' replied Omar.

'I won't ask how it was.'

Omar wasn't sure what to say to that. As he'd discovered over recent days, sometimes there was just nothing to say. He ordered another beer for Johnno.

'How's your dad?'

Omar shrugged. 'I don't know. He's not one for discussing feelings. I suppose I should be glad that at least he's talking to me now.'

'Sometimes these things bring people together.'

'I hope so.'

Johnno raised his glass. 'To your mum. Lovely lady.'

'Thanks, bro.' Omar hadn't cried during his time at home. They'd known for several months that his mother didn't have long; the lung cancer was inoperable. They'd all had time to prepare for the worst. But, for a moment, he felt as if tears might come.

The surge of emotion passed. He took a long sip of lager.

'So you do think he might come round?' asked Johnno.

'Dad? Hard to tell. The only thing that would really make him happy is if I left the army. But that's not going to happen. Honestly, I'd just settle for a chat on the phone every now and again. At least he has Nas and Dhiya.'

'They still live at home?'

'Nas does. He's only fifteen.'

'Dhiya's at uni, right?'

'Yes. Second year. Law. Dad's happy because she's only around the corner and in a house with three other Muslim girls. It was tough waving goodbye to her and Nas at the airport.' Omar realised he needed to explain. 'They've gone to Pakistan to repatriate mum's body.

It's what she and Dad wanted. They were both born in Tazagram – there's a plot there. I spoke to Dhiya this morning. The burial and ceremony all went well. They'll be flying back in a week.'

'Your dad didn't go?'

'He can't fly – remember the blood clot thing last year? I really should have gone but I haven't been back with my unit for almost five months. Can't push my luck with Major Dixon.'

'Supposed to be a bit of a hard-arse, right?'

'So they tell me. I reckon I'll be training – punishment for all this time on secondment. It's fair enough, I owe the battalion.'

'When do you have to report?'

'Day after tomorrow.'

'Well I'm on leave 'til Thursday.' Johnno held up his pint. 'Time for a few of these. Or more than a few.'

'Sounds good to me.'

They were well into their second beer when Omar's phone rang. He saw it was Dhiya and answered straight away. Stepping down off the stool, he ambled towards a nearby window.

'Dhiya, you okay?'

The panicked tone of her voice told her instantly that she wasn't.

'It's Nas. He's gone.'

'What do you mean?'

'He's gone, Omar. Somebody's taken him. You have to get here as soon as you can. Please!'

Johnno drove him over to Heathrow to catch the next available flight to Islamabad. The whole thing was surreal and yet the conversation with Dhiya had left him in no doubt. Having endured this horror himself, Omar could not believe his beleaguered family now faced yet another trial.

The car journey at least gave him some time before he was in the air and out of reach. He was able to call Dhiya back and persuade her not to tell their father about Nas. Abbas Ramay was not a well man and he had just lost his wife. During the second call, Dhiya managed to calm down a little and Omar also spoke to his uncle, the head of the family in Tazagram. Dhiya had always been a sensible, dutiful girl; Omar hoped she could hold it together until he arrived. He also had time to contact the one man in Pakistan who he knew would help him.

His name was Sajid Ansari, formerly of the SSG (Pakistani Special Forces). Omar and Sajid had met during a joint NATO-Pakistani operation near the Khyber Pass in 2013. Their convoy had come under attack from the Taliban. Sajid had been badly wounded and it was Omar who had dragged him to the safety of a nearby troop-carrier. Sajid was now a government advisor but the pair had remained friends. Sajid was fond of referring to Omar as his brother. They spoke only for five minutes but Sajid instantly volunteered to put off a family holiday and drive north to meet Omar off the plane.

The Etihad Airways Boeing 747 was in the air for eight hours. Once on Pakistani soil, Omar hoped his first call to Dhiya might yield some good news. But there was still no sign of Nas and though the family in Tazagram were doing all they could, his sister sounded even more desperate.

Sajid was waiting in a white 4X4 outside Peshawar airport. Omar threw his bag in the back and jumped in. Sajid was a large man, broad-shouldered and now a little heavier than the last time they'd met. Upon his right cheek were three scars, shrapnel wounds sustained during the Taliban attack.

Faces grim, the two old friends shook hands.

'How long?' asked Omar.

'Two hours. This thing has government plates. No one will bother us.'

Saj gunned the 4X4, dodged past a hesitant taxi and roared out of the airport.

When they arrived in Tazagram, the gates of the compound were already open. The male members of the family hurried out but were instantly overtaken by Dhiya. She threw herself at her older brother and held him tight.

'I'm so glad you're here.'

Omar squeezed her shoulder and moved forward to greet his relatives. Several branches of his family shared the compound but the most senior individual was his uncle, Usman. A portly man with a thick beard, he had done very well out of his small transportation business. Over the years, Usman had grown increasingly reticent with Omar. He and the rest of the family had very mixed feelings about the British soldier in their midst. Omar just hoped they would pull together in this hour of need.

The warmth of Usman's greetings assuaged some of his fears.

He swiftly moved on to his other uncles and aunts and introduced Sajid as 'a friend'.

Though a stranger to them, Saj's assured presence somehow seemed to smooth the way. Usman invited the new arrivals into the cool room that he used as an office. Omar, Saj and Dhiya entered along with two other uncles and Farhan, Usman's youngest son. In seconds, two aunts appeared with a pot of fresh, black tea and began filling cups.

7th Parachute Regiment RHA History.

The regiment was formed on 27 June 1961 with the re-designation of 33rd Parachute Light Regiment Royal Artillery as 7th Parachute Regiment Royal Horse Artillery. The regiment first saw action in the middle-east in Kuwait in 1961 and then in Aden in 1963–65 where it was involved in fierce fighting in the Radfan mountains. The 1970s and 80's saw the regiment involved in four Northern Ireland tours in the infantry role as well as a period where they briefly lost their airborne status and were arms-plotted to Germany until 1984 when they joined newly formed 5th Airborne Brigade and returned to Aldershot.

In 1994 the regiment deployed to Cyprus as part of the UN mission to patrol the buffer-zone between Cypriot and Turkish forces. This was followed in 1996–97 with two battery deployments to Bosnia as part of the NATO mission and the Kosovo campaign of 1999.

Since the formation of 16 Air Assault Brigade in 1999, 7 Para RHA has been involved in numerous overseas operations. The Sierra Leone campaign in summer 2000 was followed by Op Essential Harvest in Macedonia a year later. The regiment also sent a number of troops to Northern Ireland in 2001 who were at the forefront of the Holy Cross riots in that year while deployed with the 1st Battalion the Royal Irish Regiment. Two batteries deployed to the Kabul area of Afghanistan in early 2002.

On the afternoon of 19 March 2003 7 PARA fired the first shots of the Iraq War by any coalition ground forces.

The next day they crossed the border in support of the US I Marine Expeditionary Force.

The regiment was instrumental in securing the strategic Rumalya oilfields and supporting the MEF in their move north to Nasiriyah.

In late 2003 the regiment moved from Aldershot to Colchester to join the rest of 16 Air Assault Brigade. 2006 saw the first of the regiment's three tours of Afghanistan. The first of these saw the regiment play a key role in the break into Helmand province. This tour attracted much public attention and has often been described as the most intense combat fighting since the Korean War of the 1950s. The regiment returned to Helmand two years later and were again involved in heavy fighting – cumulating in the large scale operation to move a turbine from Kandahar along a heavily mined and fiercely defended road to the Kajaki Dam. 7 PARA's final deployment to Afghanistan saw the regiment's gun groups and Fire Support Teams deploy to central Helmand Province in order to provide offensive support to 16th Air Assault Brigade.

What manner of men are these who wear The Maroon Beret? They are firstly all volunteers, and are then toughened by hard physical training. As a result they have that infectious optimism and that offensive eagerness which comes from physical wellbeing. They have jumped from the air and by doing so have conquered fear. Their duty lies in the van of the battle: they are proud of this honour and have never failed in any task. They have the highest standards in all things, whether it be skill in battle or smartness in the execution of all peace time duties. They have shown themselves to be as tenacious and determined in defence as they are courageous in attack. They are, in fact, men apart - every man an Emperor.

Field Marshal Montgomery

Printed in Great Britain
by Amazon

20016401R00112